HUDSON TAYLOR'S

SPIRITUAL SECRET

By Howard and Geraldine Taylor
Edited and Revised by Gwen Hanna

OMF BOOKS

Hudson Taylor's Spiritual Secret

Copyright © 2010, OMF International

Published by OMF International. 10 West Dry Creek Circle, Littleton CO 80120

Hudson Taylor's Spiritual Secret was first published in 1932 by the China Inland Mission (Overseas Missionary Fellowship), now OMF International. This edition is based on the original text with few content revisions. It has been edited by Gwen Hanna and authorized and published by OMF International (U.S.).

ISBN-10 1-929122-32-2

ISBN-13 978-1-929122-32-5

First published 2007.

This printing 2010.

OMF BOOKS

OMF Books are distributed worldwide. Visit *www.OMFBooks.com* for more information.

CONTENTS

FOREWORD (1932)

This record has been prepared especially for readers unfamiliar with the details of Hudson Taylor's life. Those who have read the larger biography by the present writers, or Marshall Broomhall's more recent presentation, will find little that is new in these pages. But there are many, in the western world especially, who have hardly heard of Hudson Taylor, who have little time for reading and might turn away from a book in two volumes, yet who need and long for the inward joy and power that Hudson Taylor found.

The desire of the writers is to make available to busy people the experiences of their beloved father—thankful for the blessing brought to their own lives by what he was, and what he found in God, no less than by his fruitful labors.

Howard and Geraldine Taylor
Philadelphia, May 21, 1932

Men are God's method. The church is looking for better methods; God is looking for better men. ... What the church needs today is not more machinery or better, not new organizations or more and novel methods, but men whom the Holy Ghost can use—men of prayer, men mighty in prayer. The Holy Ghost does not come on machinery, but on men. He does not anoint plans, but men—men of prayer. ...

The training of the Twelve was the great, difficult and enduring work of Christ. ... It is not great talents or great learning or great preachers that God needs, but men great in holiness, great in faith, great in love, great in fidelity, great for God—men always preaching by holy sermons in the pulpit, by holy lives out of it. These can mold a generation for God.

E. M. Bounds

The founder of the China Inland Mission was a physician, J. Hudson Taylor, a man full of the Holy Ghost and of faith, of entire surrender to God and his call, of great self-denial, heartfelt compassion, rare power in prayer, marvelous organizing faculty, energetic initiative, indefatigable perseverance, and of astonishing influence with men, and withal of childlike humility.

Professor Warneck

Surely never was man better fitted for his work than he for the difficult undertaking of founding and conducting a great interdenominational and international mission in million-peopled China. The China Inland Mission was conceived in his soul, and every stage of its advance sprang from his personal exertions. In the quiet of his heart, in deep unutterable communings with God, the mission had its origin, and it remains his memorial.

H. Grattan Guinness, D.D.

CHAPTER 1

AN OPEN SECRET

Bear not a single care thyself,
One is too much for thee;
The work is Mine, and Mine alone;
Thy work—to rest in Me.
~ Selected

Hudson Taylor was a busy man, the father of a family and one who bore large responsibilities. Intensely practical, he lived a life of constant change among men of various economic and religious positions. Small in stature and far from strong, he always faced physical limitations. Next to having godly parents, the main advantage of his early years was that he had to support himself from the time he was about 16 years old. He became a hard worker and an efficient doctor; he was able to care for a baby, cook a dinner, keep financial accounts, and comfort the sick and sorrowing to the same degree that he could begin great enterprises and give spiritual leadership to thoughtful men and women all over the world.

Above all, he tested the promises of God and proved that it was possible to live a consistent spiritual life on the highest plane. He overcame difficulties which few men have ever had to encounter and left a work which more than 140 years after his death is still growing in extent and usefulness. Inland China opened to the gospel largely as an outcome of this life—tens of thousands of souls won to Christ in previously unreached provinces; nearly 1,300 missionaries depending upon God to supply all their needs without promise of salary; a mission which has never made an appeal for financial help, yet has never been in debt, that never asks anyone to join its ranks, yet at present is seeking God for 900 new members by 2011—such is the challenge that calls us to emulate Hudson Taylor's faith and devotion.

What was the secret of such a life? Hudson Taylor had many secrets, for he was always in communion with God, yet it came down to one—the simple, profound secret of drawing for every need upon "the fathomless wealth of Christ." To find out how he did this and to adopt his simple, practical attitude toward spiritual things would ease our burdens so that we too might become all that God would make us. We want, we need, and we may have Hudson Taylor's secret and his success, for we have Hudson Taylor's Bible and his God.

Remember your leaders, who spoke the word of
God to you. Consider the outcome of their way of
life and imitate their faith. Jesus Christ is the same
yesterday and today and forever. Heb. 13:7-8

CHAPTER 2

SOUL-GROWTH IN EARLY YEARS

Turn your eyes upon Jesus,
Look full in his wonderful face;
And the things of earth will grow strangely dim
In the light of his glory and grace.
~ Helen Lemmel

It all began during a quiet hour in his father's library when, as a boy, Hudson Taylor looked for something to interest him. His mother was away from home and he was missing her. The house seemed empty, so he took the story he found to a favorite corner in the old warehouse, thinking he would read it as long as it did not get dull.

Many miles away, his mother was especially burdened that Saturday afternoon about her only son. Leaving her friends, she went alone to plead with God for his salvation. She spent hour after hour on her knees until her heart was flooded with a joyful assurance that her prayers were heard and answered.

Meanwhile the boy was reading the booklet he had picked up, and as the story merged into something more serious, he was arrested by the words: "The finished work of Christ." Who can explain the mystery of the Holy Spirit's working? This truth that was very familiar, though neglected, came back to his mind and heart.

"Why does the writer use those words?" he questioned. "Why does he not say, 'the atoning or propitiatory work of Christ'?"

Immediately the words, "It is finished," jumped off the page. Finished? What was finished?

"A full and perfect atonement for sin," his heart replied. "The debt was paid by the great substitute. 'Christ died for our sins,' and 'not only for ours, but also for the sins of the whole world.'"

Then this thought came with startling clearness, "If the whole work is finished and the whole debt is paid, what is there left for me to do?"

The one and only answer took possession of his soul: "There was nothing in the world for me to do save to fall upon my knees and accepting this Savior and his salvation to praise him forevermore."

Old doubts and fears were gone. The reality of the wonderful experience we call conversion filled him with peace and joy. New life came with that simple acceptance of the Lord Jesus Christ, for to "all who received him, to those who believed in his name, he gave the right to become children of God" (John 1:12). And the change that new life brought was great.

Longing to share his newfound joy with his mother, he was the first to welcome her on her return.

"I know, my boy, I know," she said with her arms about him. "I have been rejoicing for two weeks in the glad news you have to tell."

He was in for another surprise, when, picking up a notebook he thought was his own, he found an entry in his sister's writing to the effect that she would give herself daily to prayer until God should answer in the conversion of her only brother. The young girl had recorded this decision just a month previously.

"Brought up in such a circle," Hudson Taylor wrote, "and saved under such circumstances, it was perhaps natural that from the very commencement of my Christian life I was led to feel that the promises of the Bible are very real, and that prayer is in sober fact transacting business with God, whether on one's own behalf or on behalf of those for whom one seeks his blessing."

The brother and sister were now one in a new way, and even though they were young (he was only 17), they began to do all they could to win others to Christ. This was the secret of their rapid spiritual growth. From the very first they entered into the Lord's own yearning for the lost and dying. They went out not in "social service" but in living for others with a supreme concern for their soul's salvation. This was not done with any sense of superiority, but it was simply from a deep, personal love for the Lord Jesus Christ.

As the days went by it was that love that made it so distressing to fail by acting in the old ways and lose the joy of God's conscious presence. For there were ups and downs as with most young Christians, and neglecting prayer and feeding on God's word always brings coldness of heart. But the outstanding thing about Hudson Taylor's early experience was that he could not be satisfied with anything less than the best—God's best—the real and constant enjoyment of his presence. To go without this was to live without sunlight, to work without power.

He knew the joy of the Lord in those early days as is evident from recollections such as the following. A leisurely afternoon had brought opportunity for prayer and, moved by deep longings, Hudson went to his room to be alone with God.

"Well do I remember how in the gladness of my heart I poured out my soul before God. Again and again, confessing my grateful love to him who had done everything for me, who had saved me when I had given up all hope and even desire for salvation, I besought him to give me some work to do for him as an outlet for love and gratitude. ...

"Well do I remember as I put myself, my life, my friends, my all upon the altar, the deep solemnity that came over my soul with the assurance that my offering was accepted. The presence of God became unutterable real and blessed, and I remember ... stretching myself on the ground and lying there before him with unspeakable awe and unspeakable joy. For what service I was accepted I knew not, but a deep consciousness that I was not my own took possession of me which has never since been effaced."

If we think that teenagers are too young for these kinds of experiences of the soul, we are mistaken. If the heart's deepest springs are open to the love of Christ, there is no time in life that there is greater capacity for devotion.

CHAPTER 3

FIRST STEPS OF FAITH

And evermore beside him on his way
The unseen Christ shall move;
That he may lean upon his arm and say,
"Dost Thou, dear Lord, approve?"
~ H. W. Longfellow

This sense of call did not come to a perfect person. Hudson Taylor was a normal boy living a busy life. Whether as clerk in a bank or assistant in his father's store, he had many temptations, and when a lively cousin came to be his roommate, it was not easy to keep first things first and make time for prayer. He knew, though, that without prayer there could only be failure and unrest. Taylor had to learn that there is no substitute for real spiritual blessing.

"My soul thirsts for you," was the longing of David, "my soul will be satisfied" (Ps. 63:1,5). The boy from Barnsley had the same hunger and thirst which the Lord loves to fill.

It was at a time when he was experiencing defeat and longing that the touch of God came to Hudson Taylor in a new way. In a moment and without a spoken word, he understood.

He had come to an end of himself, to a place where only God could deliver, and where he must have his aid and saving strength. If God would work on his behalf to break the power of sin, giving him inward victory in Christ, he would give up on all his earthly hopes and dreams and would go anywhere, do anything, suffer whatever might be demanded and be wholly at God's disposal. This was the cry of his heart, given while pleading with God to sanctify him and keep him from falling.

"Never shall I forget," he wrote long after, "the feeling that came over me then. Words could not describe it. I felt I was in the presence of God, entering into a covenant with the Almighty. I felt as though I wished to withdraw my promise but could not. Something seemed to say, 'Your prayer is answered; your conditions are accepted.' And from that time the conviction has never left me that I was called to China."

China had been familiar to him from childhood because of his father's focused prayers. His parents had dedicated him to that great country even before his birth. China's need and darkness had often called him—was this indeed God's purpose for his life? Distinctly, as if a voice had spoken, the word came in the silence, "Then go for me to China."

From that moment, Taylor's life was unified in one great purpose and prayer. Hudson Taylor "was not disobedient to the vision from heaven" (Acts 26:19). To him, obedience to the will of God was a very practical matter. At once he began to prepare for a life that would call for physical endurance. He exercised more, exchanged his feather bed for a hard mattress and was careful with his diet. Instead of going to church twice on Sunday, he gave up the evening service to visit the poorest parts of the town to distribute tracts and hold gatherings in people's homes. He became a welcome figure in crowded lodging-house kitchens, and his bright face and kind words opened the way for many to hear the gospel. All of this led to more Bible study and more time in prayer, because the opportunities showed him all the more that only God can make us "fishers of men" (Matt. 4:19).

Taylor also began an intense study of the Chinese language. He could not afford the language book that would cost more than $20 nor the dictionary which would be at least $75. Instead he patiently compared brief verses from a copy of the Gospel of Luke in Chinese with their equivalent in English. He found out the meaning of more than 600 characters which he learned and made into a dictionary of his own.

"I have begun," he wrote to his sister at school, "to get up at five in the morning, and find it necessary to go to bed early. I must study if I mean to go to China. I am fully decided to go, and am making every preparation I can. I intend to rub up my Latin, to learn Greek and the rudiments of Hebrew, and get as much general information as possible. I need your prayers."

Taylor spent several years working with his father as a pharmacist which increased his desire to study medicine. When God opened the way, he jumped at the opportunity to become an assistant to a leading physician in Hull. This meant leaving his home, but he found comfortable accommodations, first in the doctor's residence and later in the home of an aunt.

This comfort proved to be an aspect of his new life that challenged him. Dr. Hardey paid enough salary to cover personal expenses, but as a matter of duty and privilege, Hudson Taylor was giving a tenth of all that came to him to the work of God. He was devoting time on Sunday to evangelism in a very needy part of town which raised the question, "Why shouldn't he spend less for himself and have the joy of giving more to others?"

On the outskirts of the town, beyond some vacant lots, a double row of cottages bordered a narrow canal. This unattractive neighborhood was known as "Drainside." The canal was a deep ditch into which the people of Drainside were in the habit of throwing their garbage. Since Hull is a seaport town, the garbage was then carried away whenever the tide rose high enough. The cottages, like peas in a pod, followed the windings of the drain for half a mile or so. Hudson Taylor left his aunt's pleasant home on Charlotte Street to rent one of these little places which boasted just one door and two windows. His landlady, Mrs. Finch, was a true Christian and loved having "the young doctor" under her roof. She did her best to make the room clean and comfortable by polishing the fireplace opposite the window and making up the bed in the corner farthest from the door. The room was only 12 feet square and did not need much furniture so a small table and a chair or two filled the space. Being level with the ground, the room opened out of the kitchen. From the window Taylor looked across to "The Founder's Arms," a pub whose lights shown across the mud and water of the drain on dark nights.

While it may have been nicer in the summer, Drainside must have seemed quite dreary toward the close of November when Hudson Taylor made it his home. In addition to the move, Taylor was now boarding himself which meant that he needed to buy his meager supplies as he returned from work each day. He rarely sat down to a proper meal. He often walked and spent his evenings alone, and Sundays he worked long hours in his district or among the crowds who frequented the Humber Dock. He recalled:

"Having now the twofold object in view," he recalled, "of accustoming myself to endure hardness, and of economizing in order to help those among whom I was laboring in the gospel, I soon found that I could live upon very much less than I had previously thought possible. Butter, milk and other luxuries I ceased to use, and found that by living mainly on oatmeal and rice, with occasional variations, a very small sum was sufficient for my needs. In this way I had more than two-thirds of my income available for other purposes, and my experience was that the less I spent on myself and the more I gave to others, the fuller of happiness and blessing did my soul become."

In his solitude Hudson Taylor was learning something about how close God can be to the one who follows hard after him. In these days of easy-going Christianity, it is good to remind ourselves that it really does cost to be a person whom God can use. One cannot become Christlike in character without cost. Christlike work is done at great price. As Christ himself said, "Can you drink the cup I drink or be baptized with the baptism I am baptized with?" (Mark 10:38).

During this time the remarkable developments of the Taiping Rebellion* in China were occupying public attention. Many were praying and countless hearts were stirred about evangelizing that great nation. But when efforts failed to turn the tide and disappointment came, the majority stopped even caring. Prayer meetings dwindled to nothing, would-be missionaries turned to other callings, and contributions dropped off to such an extent that a number of mission societies actually ceased to exist. But the Lord could count on a few here and there—poor, weak, unknown, and unimportant, but ready, by grace, to go all lengths in carrying out his purposes.

In his quiet lodging at Drainside was such a man. With all his limitations, Hudson Taylor wholeheartedly desired to live with a Christlike character. As test after test bore down on him, he chose the pathway of self-emptying and the cross, not from any idea of that he would gain from it, but simply because he was led by the Spirit of God. He chose an attitude that allowed God to work instead of hindering any blessing.

"I know your deeds. See, I have placed before you an open door that no one can shut. I know that you have little strength, yet you have kept my word and have not denied my name" (Rev. 3:8).

"Because a great door for effective work has opened to me, and there are many who oppose me" (1 Cor. 16:9).

There were certainly many opposed to Hudson Taylor's progress at this time. He was entering one of the most fruitful periods of his life, rich in blessing for himself and others. Is it any wonder that the tempter was at hand? He was alone, hungry for love and sympathy and living a life of self-denial that was not easy to bear. It was just the opportunity for the devil, and he was permitted for a while to do his worst.

When he had been at Drainside only a few weeks he was dealt a terrible blow. The one he loved passionately seemed lost to him forever. For two long years he had hoped and waited. The uncertainty of the future made him long all the more for her presence and companionship. But now the dream was over. Seeing that nothing could dissuade her friend from his missionary purpose, the young music teacher—with her sweet face and lovely voice—made it plain at last that she was not prepared to go to China. Her father would not hear of it, nor did she feel fitted for such a life. Taylor was left with a broken heart.

"Is it all worthwhile?" urged the tempter. "Why should you go to China, after all? Why work hard and suffer all your life for an ideal of duty? Give it up now, while you can yet win her. Earn a proper living like everybody else, and serve the Lord at home. For you can win her yet."

Love pleaded hard. It was a moment of wavering. The enemy came in like a flood. Numbed with sorrow, he kept it to himself and nursed his grief instead of turning to the Lord for comfort. But he was not left alone.

"Alone in the surgery," he wrote the following day, "I had a melting season. I was thoroughly softened and humble, and had a wonderful manifestation of the love of God. A broken and contrite heart [Ps. 51:17] he did not despise, but answered my cry for blessing in very deed and truth.

"Yes, he has humbled me and shown me what I am, revealing himself as a present, a very present help in time of trouble. [See Ps. 46:1.] And though he does not deprive me of feeling in my trial, he enables me to sing, 'Yet will I rejoice in the Lord, I will joy in the God of my salvation' [Hab. 3:18]. ...

"Now I am happy in my Savior's love. I can thank him for all, even the most painful experiences of the past, and trust him without fear for all that is to come."

CHAPTER 4

FURTHER STEPS OF FAITH

Who trust in God's unchanging love
Builds on the rock that nought can move.
~ Georg Neumark, 1641,
Hymn "If You Will Only Let God Guide You"

"I never made a sacrifice," Hudson Taylor said in later years, looking back over a life in which most would see exactly the opposite. But what he said was true. He had learned through all his experience that what he gained was real and lasting and that "giving up" is inevitably receiving when one is dealing heart to heart with God. That winter living in Drainside revealed this clearly. He had accepted the will of God both inwardly and outwardly, giving up what seemed his best and highest, the love that had become his very life, so that he could follow Christ without any hindrances. The sacrifice was great, but the reward was far greater.

"Unspeakable joy," he wrote, "all day long and every day, was my happy experience. God, even my God, was a living bright reality, and all I had to do was joyful service."

Taylor's letters took on a new tone. They were less introspective and more full of missionary purpose. China came to the front again in all his thinking.

"Do not let anything unsettle you, dear Mother," he wrote about this time. "Missionary work is indeed the noblest any mortal can engage in. We certainly cannot be insensible to the ties of nature, but should we not rejoice when we have anything we can give up for the Savior? ...

"Continue to pray for me. Though comfortable as regards temporal matters, and happy and thankful, I feel I need your prayers. ... Oh, Mother, I cannot tell you, I cannot describe how I long to be a missionary; to carry the glad tidings to poor, perishing sinners; to spend and be spent for him who died for me! ... Think, Mother, of 12 million—a number so great that it is impossible to realize it— yes, 12 million souls in China, every year, passing without God and without hope into eternity. ... Oh, let us look with compassion on this multitude! God has been merciful to us; let us be like him. ...

"I must conclude. Would you not give up all for Jesus who died for you? Yes, Mother, I know you would. God be with you and comfort you. Must I leave as soon as I can save money enough to go? I feel as if I could not live if something is not done for China."

However, as much as he longed to go immediately, there were issues to consider that held him back. The little room at Drainside witnessed many internal conflicts and victory known to God alone.

"To me it was a very grave matter," he wrote of that winter, "to contemplate going out to China, far from all human aid, there to depend upon the living God alone for protection, supplies and help of every kind. I felt that one's spiritual muscles required strengthening for such an undertaking. There was no doubt that if faith did not fail, God would not fail. But what if one's faith should prove insufficient? I had not at that time learned that even 'if we believe not, yet he abideth faithful; he cannot deny himself' [2 Tim. 2:13]. It was consequently a very serious matter to my mind, not whether he was faithful, but whether I had strong enough faith to warrant my embarking on the enterprise set before me.

"'When I get out to China,' I thought to myself, 'I shall have no claim on anyone for anything. My only claim will be on God. How important to learn, before leaving England, to move man, through God, by prayer alone.'"

He was willing to pay the price for this, whatever it might be. There may have been some lack of judgment, perhaps some going to extremes, but God understood and met him wonderfully! "To move man, through God, by prayer alone"—it was a great ambition, gloriously realized that lonely winter at Drainside.

He continued, "At Hull my kind employer wished me to remind him whenever my salary became due. This I determined not to do directly, but to ask that God would bring the fact to his recollection, and thus encourage me by answering prayer.

"At one time, as the day drew near for the payment of a quarter's salary, I was as usual much in prayer about it. The time arrived, but Dr. Hardey made no allusion to the matter. I continued praying. Days passed on and he did not remember, until at length on settling up my weekly accounts one Saturday night, I found myself possessed of only one remaining coin—a half-crown piece. Still, I had hitherto known no lack, and I continued praying.

"That Sunday was a very happy one. As usual my heart was full and brimming over with blessing. After attending divine service in the morning, my afternoons and evenings were taken up with gospel work in the various lodging-houses I was accustomed to visit in the lowest part of the town. At such times it almost seemed to me as if heaven were begun below, and that all that could be looked for was an enlargement of one's capacity for joy, not a truer filling than I possessed.

"After concluding my last service about 10 o'clock that night, a poor man asked me to go and pray with his wife, saying that she was dying. I readily agreed, and on the way asked him why he had not sent for the priest, as his accent told me he was an Irishman. He had done so, he said, but the priest refused to come without a payment of 18 pence, which the man did not possess as the family was starving. Immediately it occurred to my mind that all the money I had in the world was the solitary half-crown, and that it was in one coin; moreover, that while the basin of water-gruel I usually took for supper was awaiting me, and there was sufficient in the house for breakfast in the morning, I certainly had nothing for dinner on the coming day.

"Somehow or other there was at once a stoppage in the flow of joy in my heart. But instead of reproving myself I began to reprove the poor man, telling him that it was very wrong to have allowed matters to get into such a state as he described, and that he ought to have applied to the relieving officer. His answer was that he had done so, and was told to come at 11 o'clock the next morning, but that he feared his wife might not live through the night.

"'Ah,' thought I, 'if only I had two shillings and a sixpence instead of this half-crown, how gladly would I give these poor people a shilling!' But to part with the half-crown was far from my thoughts. I little dreamed that the truth of the matter simply was that I could trust God plus one-and-sixpence, but was not prepared to trust him only, without any money at all in my pocket.

"My conductor led me into a court, down which I followed him with some degree of nervousness. I had found myself there before, and at my last visit had been roughly handled. ... Up a miserable flight of stairs into a wretched room he led me, and oh, what a sight there presented itself! Four or five children stood about, their sunken cheeks and temples telling unmistakably the story of slow starvation, and lying on a wretched pallet was a poor, exhausted mother, with a tiny infant who was only 36 hours old moaning, rather than crying, at her side.

"'Ah,' thought I, 'if I had two shillings and a sixpence, instead of half-a-crown, how gladly should they have one-and-sixpence of it.' But still a wretched unbelief prevented me from obeying the impulse to relieve their distress at the cost of all I possessed.

"It will scarcely seem strange that I was unable to say much to comfort these poor people. I needed comfort myself. I began to tell them, however, that they must not be cast down; that though their circumstances were very distressing there was a kind and loving father in heaven. But something within me cried, 'You hypocrite! Telling these unconverted people about a kind and loving father in heaven, and not prepared yourself to trust him without half-a-crown.'

"I nearly choked. How gladly would I have compromised with conscience, if I had had a florin and a sixpence! I would have given the florin thankfully and kept the rest. But I was not yet prepared to trust in God alone, without the sixpence.

"To talk was impossible under these circumstances, yet strange to say I thought I should have no difficulty in praying. Prayer was a delightful occupation in those days. Time thus spent never seemed wearisome and I knew no lack of words. I seemed to think that all I should have to do would be to kneel down and pray, and that relief would come to them and to myself together.

"'You asked me to come and pray with your wife,' I said to the man, 'let us pray.' And I knelt down.

"But no sooner had I opened my lips with, 'Our father who art in heaven,' than conscience said within, 'Dare you mock God? Dare you kneel down and call him 'father' with that half-crown in your pocket?'

"Such a time of conflict then came upon me as I had never experienced before. How I got through that form of prayer I know not, and whether the words uttered were connected or disconnected. But I arose from my knees in great distress of mind.

"The poor father turned to me and said, 'You see what a terrible state we are in, sir. If you can help us, for God's sake do!'

"At that moment the word flashed into my mind, 'Give to him that asketh of thee,' and in the word of a king there is power.

"I put my hand into my pocket and slowly drawing out the half-crown gave it to the man, telling him that it might seem a small matter for me to relieve them, seeing that I was comparatively well off, but that in parting with that coin I was giving him my all; but that what I had been trying to tell them was indeed true, God really was a father and might be trusted. And how the joy came back in full flood tide to my heart! I could say anything and feel it then, and the hindrance to blessing was gone—gone, I trust, forever.

"Not only was the poor woman's life saved, but my life as I fully realized had been saved too. It might have been a wreck—would have been, probably, as a Christian life—had not grace at that time conquered and the striving of God's Spirit been obeyed.

"I well remember that night as I went home to my lodgings how my heart was as light as my pocket. The dark, deserted streets resounded with a hymn of praise that I could not restrain. When I took my basin of gruel before retiring, I would not have exchanged it for a prince's feast. Reminding the Lord as I knelt at my bedside of his own word, 'he that giveth to the poor lendeth to the Lord' [Prov. 19:17]. I asked him not to let my loan be a long one, or I should have no dinner the next day. And with peace within and peace without, I spent a happy, restful night.

"Next morning, my plate of porridge remained for breakfast, and before it was finished the postman's knock was heard at the door. I was not in the habit of receiving letters on Monday, as my parents and most of my friends refrained from posting on Saturday, so that I was somewhat surprised when the landlady came in holding a letter or packet in her wet hand covered by her apron. I looked at the letter, but could not make out the handwriting. It was either a strange hand or a feigned one, and the postmark was blurred. Where it came from I could not tell. On opening the envelope I found nothing written within, but inside a sheet of blank paper was folded a pair of kid gloves from which, as I opened them in astonishment, half-a-sovereign fell to the ground.

"'Praise the Lord,' I exclaimed, '400 percent for a 12 hours' investment! How glad the merchants of Hull would be if they could lend their money at such a rate of interest!' Then and there I determined that a bank that could not break should have my savings or earnings as the case might be, a determination I have not yet learned to regret.

"I cannot tell you how often my mind has recurred to this incident, or all the help it has been to me in circumstances of difficulty. If we are faithful to God in little things, we shall gain experience and strength that will be helpful to us in the more serious trials of life."

But this was not the end of the story, nor was it the only answer to prayer that was to confirm Hudson Taylor's faith at this time.

"This remarkable and gracious deliverance was a great joy to me as well as a strong confirmation of faith. But of course 10 shillings, however economically used, will not go very far, and it was nonetheless necessary to continue in prayer, asking that the larger supply which was still due might be remembered and paid. All my petitions, however, appeared to remain unanswered, and before a fortnight elapsed I found myself pretty much in the same position that I had occupied on the Sunday night already made so memorable. Meanwhile I continued pleading with God, more and more earnestly, that he would himself remind Dr. Hardey that my salary was due.

"Of course it was not want of money that distressed me. That could have been had at any time for the asking. The question uppermost in my mind was, 'Can I go to China, or will my want of faith and power with God prove so serious an obstacle as to preclude my entering upon this much-prized service?'

"As the week drew to a close I felt exceedingly embarrassed. There was not only myself to consider. On Saturday night a payment would be due to my Christian landlady, which I knew she could not well dispense with. Ought I not, for her sake, to speak about the matter of the salary? Yet to do so would be, to myself at any rate, the admission that I was not fitted to undertake a missionary enterprise. I gave nearly the whole of Thursday and Friday, all the time not occupied in my necessary employment, to earnest wrestling with God in prayer. But still on Saturday morning I was in the same position as before. And now my earnest cry was for guidance as to whether I should still continue to wait the father's time. As far as I could judge, I received the assurance that to wait his time was best, and that God in some way or other would interpose on my behalf. So I waited, my heart being now at rest and the burden gone.

"About five o'clock that Saturday afternoon, when Dr. Hardey had finished writing his prescriptions, his last circuit for the day being done, he threw himself back in his armchair as he was wont and began to speak of the things of God. He was a truly Christian man, and many seasons of happy fellowship we had together. I was busily watching at the time a pan in which a decoction was boiling that required a good deal of attention. It was indeed fortunate for me that it was so, for without any obvious connection with what had been going on, all at once he said: 'By the by, Taylor, is not your salary due again?'

"My emotion may be imagined. I had to swallow two or three times before I could answer. With my eye fixed on the pan and my back to the doctor, I told him as quietly as I could that it was overdue some little time. How thankful I felt at that moment! God surely had heard my prayer and caused him in this time of my great need to remember the salary, without any word or suggestion from me.

"'Oh, I am so sorry you did not remind me,' he replied. 'You know how busy I am. I wish I had thought of it a little sooner, for only this afternoon I sent all the money I had to the bank. Otherwise I would pay you at once.'

"It was impossible to describe the revulsion of feeling caused by this unexpected statement. I knew not what to do. Fortunately for me the pan boiled up and I had a good reason for rushing with it from the room. Glad indeed I was to keep out of sight until after Dr. Hardey had returned to his house, and most thankful that he had not perceived my emotion.

"As soon as he was gone, I had to seek my little sanctum and pour out my heart before the Lord before calmness, and more than calmness, thankfulness and joy were restored. I felt that God had his own way and was not going to fail me. I had sought to know his will early in the day, and as far as I could judge had received guidance to wait patiently. And now God was going to work for me in some other way.

"That evening was spent, as my Saturday evenings usually were, in reading the word and preparing the subject on which I was expected to speak in the various lodging-houses on the morrow. I waited perhaps a little longer than usual. At last about 10 o'clock, there being no interruption of any kind, I put on my overcoat and was preparing to leave for home, rather thankful to know that by that time I should have to let myself in with the latchkey, as my landlady retired early. There was certainly no help for that night. But perhaps God would interpose for me by Monday, and I might be able to pay my landlady early in the week the money I would have given her before, had it been possible.

"Just as I was about to turn down the gas, I heard the doctor's step in the garden that lay between the dwelling-house and surgery. He was laughing to himself heartily, as though greatly amused. Entering the surgery he asked for the ledger, and told me that, strange to say, one of his richest patients had just come to pay his doctor's bill. Was it not an odd thing to do! It never struck me that it might have any bearing on my own case, or I might have felt embarrassed. Looking at it simply from the position of an uninterested spectator, I also was highly amused that a man rolling in wealth should come after 10 o'clock at night to pay a bill which he could any day have met by a check with the greatest ease. It appeared that, somehow or other, he could not rest with this on his mind, and had been constrained to come at that unusual hour to discharge his liability.

"The account was duly receipted in the ledger and Dr. Hardey was about to leave, when suddenly he turned and handing me some of the banknotes just received, said to my surprise and thankfulness: 'By the by, Taylor, you might as well take these notes. I have no change, but can give you the balance next week.'

"Again I was left, my feelings undiscovered, to go back to my little closet and praise the Lord with a joyful heart that after all I might go to China."

CHAPTER 5

FAITH TRIED AND STRENGTHENED

Enough that God my Father knows:—
Nothing this faith can dim.
He gives the very best to those
Who leave the choice with him.
~ Selected

"After all, I might go to China!" But so many testings were still ahead. If his life was to be exceptionally fruitful, it had to be rooted and grounded in God in extraordinary ways.

After his time in Hull, Hudson Taylor went to London where he entered as a medical student at one of the hospitals. He was still depending on the Lord alone for supplies, even though both his father and the Chinese Evangelization Society, which ultimately sent him to China, offered to help with his expenses. He was determined to continue to test the promises of God. When he turned down his father's generous offer, friends at home concluded that the society was meeting his needs. While the society did cover his fees at the London hospital and an uncle in Soho gave him a home for a few weeks, there was nothing except the faithfulness of God to provide for his needs.

Before leaving Hull he had written to his mother, "I am indeed proving the truth of that word, 'Thou wilt keep him in perfect peace whose mind is stayed on thee, because he trusteth in thee' [Is. 26:3]. My mind is quite as much at rest as, nay more than, it would be if I had 100 pounds in my pocket. May he keep me ever thus, simply depending on him for every blessing, temporal as well as spiritual."

And to his sister Amelia he wrote, "No situation has turned up in London that will suit me, but I am not concerned about it, as he is 'the same yesterday, and today and forever' [Heb. 13:8]. His love is unfailing, his word unchangeable, his power ever the same; therefore the heart that trusts him is kept in 'perfect peace.' ... I know he tries me only to increase my faith, and that it is all in love. Well, if he is glorified, I am content."

Hudson Taylor had one all-sufficient confidence for his future. If that could fail, it was better to make that discovery in London rather than far away in China. Deliberately and of his own free will, he cut himself off from all possible sources of supply. It was the living God he needed—a stronger faith to grasp his faithfulness and more experience practicing trust in every situation. Compared with deeper knowledge of God on whom everything depends, comfort or discomfort in London and means or the lack of means seemed like small concerns. Now that he had further opportunity to put that knowledge to the test, he did not hesitate, even though he knew that a great trial would likely be involved.

The outcome proved that in this decision, he was indeed led of God. There were many and unmistakable answers to prayer in London. This strengthened his faith and gave just the preparation he needed for unforeseen developments which sped up his departure for China to within the next 12 months. In his own brief Retrospect [now published as Looking Back], Hudson Taylor tells the story of these experiences. It is enough to say here that he suffered loneliness and lacked many comforts. This test of endurance—when for months he lived on nothing but brown bread and apples, walked more than eight miles a day to and from the hospital—and all the uncertainty as to his connection with the one and only society prepared to send him to China without university training, went far to make him the man of faith he was even at this early age.

Hudson Taylor was only 21 when the way opened unexpectedly and he was requested by the Chinese Evangelization Society to sail for Shanghai as soon as a vessel could be found. The Taiping Rebellion was pressing forward successfully. With its capital firmly established at Nanking, its nominally Christian forces had swept over the central and northern provinces, and Peking itself was almost within their grasp. "Send me teachers, many teachers to help in making known the truth," wrote Hung Hsiu-ch'uan, founder of the Taiping movement, to an American missionary. "Hereafter, when my enterprise is successfully terminated, I will disseminate the doctrine throughout the whole empire, that all may return to the one Lord and worship the true God only. This is what my heart earnestly desires."

It seemed as though China would be thrown open to messengers of the gospel. Christian hearts everywhere were deeply moved. Something must be done and done at once to meet so great a crisis, and, for a time, money poured in. Among other projects, the British and Foreign Bible Society celebrated its jubilee by printing a million copies of the Chinese New Testament, and the society with which Hudson Taylor was in correspondence decided to send two men to Shanghai for work in the interior. One of these, a Scottish physician, could not leave immediately, but they counted on the younger man, Hudson Taylor, to go at short notice, even though it meant sacrificing the degrees he was working for in medicine and surgery.

It was a serious step to take, and Taylor naturally turned to his parents for counsel and prayer. After an interview with Mr. Bird, one of the secretaries of the Chinese Evangelization Society, he wrote to his mother, "Mr. Bird has removed most of the difficulties I have been feeling, and I think it will be well to comply with his suggestion and at once propose myself to the committee. I shall await your answer, and rely upon your prayers. If I should be accepted to go at once, would you advise me to come home before sailing? I long to be with you once more, and I know you would naturally wish to see me; but I almost think it would be easier for us not to meet, than having met to part again forever. No, not forever!

> *"A little while: 'twill soon be past!*
> *Why should we shun the promised cross?*
> *Oh, let us in his footsteps haste,*
> *Counting for him all else but loss:*
> *Then, how will recompense his smile*
> *The sufferings of this little while!*

"I cannot write more, but hope to hear from you as soon as possible. Pray much for me. It is easy to talk of leaving all for Christ, but when it comes to the proof—it is only as we stand 'complete in him' we can go through with it. God be with you and bless you, my own dear Mother, and give you so to realize the preciousness of Jesus that you may wish for nothing but 'to know him' ... even in 'the fellowship of his sufferings' [Phil. 3:10]."

And to his sister he wrote, "Pray for me, dear Amelia, that he who has promised to meet all our need may be with me in this painful though long-expected hour. When we look at ourselves, at the littleness of our love, the barrenness of our service and the small progress we make toward perfection, how soul-refreshing it is to turn away to him; to plunge afresh in 'the fountain opened ... for sin and for uncleanness' [Zech. 13:1]; to remember that we are 'accepted in the beloved' [Eph. 1:6] ... 'who of God is made unto us wisdom, and righteousness, and sanctification, and redemption' [1 Cor. 1:30]. Oh! The fullness of Christ, the fullness of Christ."

Hudson Taylor first reached the shores of China in 1854 after a perilous voyage of five months. At that time there were many restrictions on evangelism. Shanghai and four other treaty ports were the only places where foreigners could live, and there wasn't a single Protestant missionary anywhere in the interior, away from the coast. Civil war was raging, and the Taiping propaganda had begun to lose its earlier characteristics. Already it was degenerating into the corrupt political movement which deluged the country with blood and sufferings during the remaining 11 years of its course. Instead of being able to reach Nanking, Hudson Taylor had the greatest difficulty in gaining a foothold even in Shanghai. Travel to other locations was very risky.

Years afterwards, when he was responsible for the guidance of many missionaries, it was easy for Taylor to see that the trials of those early days were all needed. Even though neither he nor others could imagine it, he was pioneering a way in China for hundreds who were to follow. He needed every burden and the experience of every test to prepare him. As iron is tempered to steel, his heart needed to be stronger and more patient than others, and that came through having loved and suffered more. In order to encourage thousands in a life of childlike trust, he needed to learn the deeper lessons of his father's loving care. So, especially at first when impressions are deep and lasting, Taylor faced many difficulties. God's deliverance from many of them made them a lifelong blessing.

To begin with, Shanghai was in the grip of war. A band of rebels known as the "Red Turbans" controlled the city, close to the foreign settlement, and 40-50,000 of the national forces were encamped around it. Fighting was almost continuous, and the foreign militia was called out frequently to protect the settlement. Everything was at famine prices, and both the city and settlement were so crowded one could scarcely find accommodations for any price. Had it not been that Dr. William Lockhart of the London mission was able to house him for a time,

Taylor would have had a very difficult time finding lodging. Even so, he could see sharp fighting from his windows, and he was unable to walk in any direction without witnessing unthinkable misery.

It was also bitterly cold when Hudson Taylor first reached Shanghai, and as coal was selling at $50 a ton, it was not possible to do much to warm the houses. He was not accustomed to luxuries and was thankful for a shelter anywhere ashore, but he suffered in the penetrating chill and damp.

"My position is a very difficult one," he wrote soon after his arrival. "Dr. Lockhart has taken me to reside with him for the present, as houses are not to be had for love or money. ... No one can live in the city. ... They are fighting now while I write, and the house shakes with the report of cannon.

"It is so cold that I can hardly think or hold the pen. You will see from my letter to Mr. [Edward] Pearse [a representative of the mission society] how perplexed I am. It will be four months before I can hear in reply, and the very kindness of the missionaries who have received me with open arms makes me fear to be burdensome. Jesus will guide me aright. ... I love the Chinese more than ever. Oh, to be useful among them!"

Of his first Sunday in China he wrote, "I attended two services at the London mission and in the afternoon went into the city with Mr. Wylie. You have never seen a city in a state of siege. ... God grant you never may! We walked some distance round the wall, and sad it was to see the wreck of rows upon rows of houses. Burnt down, blown down, battered to pieces—in all stages of ruin they were! And the misery of those who once occupied them and now, at this inclement season, are driven from home and shelter is terrible to think of. ...

"By the time we came to the north gate they were fighting fiercely outside the city. One man was carried in dead, another shot through the chest, and a third whose arm I examined seemed in dreadful agony. A ball had gone clean through the arm breaking the bone in passing. ... A little farther on we met some men bringing in a small cannon they had captured, and following them were others dragging along by their tails [queues] five wretched prisoners. The poor fellows cried to us piteously to save them as they were hurried by, but alas, we could do nothing! They would probably be at once decapitated. It makes one's blood run cold to think of such things."

The sufferings of those around him, and the fact that he could do little or nothing to help, would have been overwhelming, except for the strength God poured through him.

"What it means to be so far from home, at the seat of war," he added, "and not able to understand or be understood by the people was fully realized. Their utter wretchedness and misery and my inability to help them or even point them to Jesus powerfully affected me. Satan came in as a flood, but there was one who lifted up a standard against him. Jesus is here, and though unknown to the majority and uncared-for by many who might know him, he is present and precious to his own."

He faced personal trials as well. For the first time in his life, Hudson Taylor found himself in a position in which he could hardly meet his financial obligations. He had willingly lived on next to nothing at home, to keep within his means, but now he could not avoid expenses altogether beyond his income. Living with others who were receiving three or four times his salary, he was obliged to board as they did and he watched his limited resources rapidly melt away. At home he had been a collector for foreign missions, and he knew what it was to receive the meager contributions of the poor. Missionary money was to him a sacred trust, and to have to use it so freely caused him real distress. He wrote letters to the society but the replies he received were unsatisfactory. After waiting months for instructions, he might hear nothing at all in answer to his most urgent questions. The committee in London was far away and little able to understand his circumstances. They were mostly busy men, absorbed in their own affairs. Even with the best intentions and a real desire to forward the work of God, they were unable to visualize a situation so different from anything they had ever known. Hudson Taylor did his best to make matters clear to them, but month after month went by and he was left in uncertainty and financial distress.

The Shanghai dollar, previously worth about 50 cents gold, was up to double that and continually rising higher, yet it had no more purchasing value. Because it cost more just for the necessities of life than he earned in his salary, he made use of a letter of credit provided against emergencies. He could not, however, obtain any assurance that his bills would be honored. For one so conscientious in money matters, this was a painful situation that kept him awake many nights.

The heat of summer added more perplexities. Not from his own committee, but in a roundabout way Hudson Taylor learned that the Scottish physician who was to be his colleague had already sailed from England with his wife and children. He had not received any instructions about how to find housing for the family, and as the weeks went by, he realized that unless he took steps in the matter they would be left without a roof over their heads. Without authorization to spend the funds necessary, he had to find and rent rooms of some sort for five people. This was no easy task. Not wanting to spend the money on a sedan chair—the proper means of transport—he spent himself in the blinding heat of August searching all through city and settlement for houses that were not to be had. His Shanghai friends assured him that the only thing to do was to buy land and build immediately. How could he tell them the true situation or reveal his lack of funds? The community was already critical about the management of the society he represented, so he had to keep his troubles to himself, as far as possible, and seek to cast his burden upon the Lord.

"One who is really leaning on the Beloved," he wrote under the circumstances, "finds it always possible to say, 'I will fear no evil, for thou art with me' [Ps. 23:4]. But I am so apt, like Peter, to take my eyes off the one to be trusted and look at the winds and waves. ... Oh for more stability! The reading of the word and meditation on the promises have been increasingly precious to me of late. At first I allowed my desire to acquire the language speedily to have undue prominence and a deadening effect on my soul. But now, in the grace that passes all understanding, the Lord has again caused his face to shine upon me."

And to his sister he added, "I have been puzzling my brains again about a house, etc., but to no effect. So I have made it a matter of prayer and have given it entirely into the Lord's hands, and now I feel quite at peace about it. He will provide and be my guide in this and every other perplexing step."

It must have seemed almost too good to be true when, only two days after the above was written, Hudson Taylor heard of a house that could be rented. Before the month was over, he had a house large enough to accommodate his expected colleagues. Five rooms upstairs and seven down seemed indeed a spacious residence. And though it was only a poor Chinese place, built of wood and likely to fall to pieces, it was among the people, near the north gate of the city. This is where he established himself six months after his arrival in China. Though the situation was so dangerous that his teacher did not dare to go with him, he was able to engage a Shanghai Christian, an educated man, who could help him learn the local dialect.

Hudson Taylor found great joy in being among the Chinese in a place of his own, and able, with the help of his new teacher, to carry on daily meetings and do a good deal of medical work. But the location proved more perilous than he had anticipated. It was beyond the protection of the settlement and within range of the Imperial artillery constantly covering the north gate. It was not difficult to discover why the house had been left vacant. For almost three months the young missionary was able to hold on in the hope of some change for the better. But then the situation became desperate. His life had been in danger repeatedly, and day after day he witnessed scenes of terrible cruelty. Finally the house next door was set on fire in order to drive out the foreigner. He had no choice but to go back to the London mission. He found a refuge there, just in time for the arrival of Dr. George Parker and his family.

A little house on the London Missionary Society property, close to Dr. Lockhart's, had been the home of Hudson Taylor's dearest friends in China, Mr. and Mrs. John Burdon. He had often enjoyed their fireside conversations, rejoicing in the happiness of the young English missionary and his wife. But when Mrs. Burdon died during the birth of their first child, Mr. Burdon had taken his motherless little one to the care of fellow workers. In his sorrow for his friend, Hudson Taylor had not realized how the empty house so rich in memories would affect his own situation. But before he had to leave his dangerous location near the north gate, the Burdon home was for rent. The arrival of the Parkers was expected daily, and though it left him with only three dollars in hand, Taylor secured the house, just in time to receive his colleagues, including a baby born at sea.

To help the situation, he was glad to sublet half the house to another missionary family in distress, but that left only three rooms for the Parkers and himself. He had so few belongings, that he could not furnish the place well for six people. But this was only the beginning of troubles. After the long voyage, Dr. Parker, too, had only a few dollars in hand, and he was depending on a letter of credit from the mission society, which by some mistake did not turn up. It was supposed to have been sent off before the Parkers left England, but month after month went by and there was no word of it. The family was not expecting such a severe winter, and they were desperately in need of warmer clothing and bedding. It is hard to imagine how they lived through all those months in such conditions.

Quietly Dr. and Mrs. Parker held on, not turned aside from their missionary work by the tempting possibilities open to a medical man in Shanghai. He went out regularly with Taylor to evangelize in the city and surrounding villages, and at home in their crowded quarters they devoted themselves to study. But all this burned lessons into Hudson Taylor's heart of how not to deal with those who, on the human side, are dependent on one's care. Several of the members of the committee in London were dear, personal friends of the missionaries. They had shared memorable fellowship in spiritual things, and even when feeling their mistakes most keenly, Hudson Taylor longed for their atmosphere of prayer and love for the word of God. But something somehow was missing. The young missionary had to discover what it was so that he could be practical as well as spiritual in his leadership in the days to come. These lessons were difficult to learn, but the years to come provided what he needed in many situations.

"You ask how I get over my troubles," he wrote to his sister and intimate correspondent. "This is the way. ... I take them to the Lord. Since writing the above, I have been reading my evening portion— Psalms 72 to 74. Read them and see how applicable they are. I don't know how it is, but I can seldom read Scripture now without tears of joy and gratitude. ...

"I see that to be as I am and have been since my arrival has really been more conducive to improvement and progress than any other position would have been, though in many respects it has been painful and far from what I should myself have chosen. Oh, for more implicit reliance on the wisdom and love of God!"

CHAPTER 6

FRIENDSHIP AND SOMETHING MORE

Love that bent low beneath his brother's burden,
How shall he soar and find all sorrows flown!
Love that ne'er asked for answer or for guerdon,
How shall he meet eyes sweeter than his own!
~ F. W. H. Meyers

Nothing in the records of his first two years in China is more surprising than the way in which Hudson Taylor devoted himself to pioneer evangelism. One might have thought that with the study of the language, living in war conditions and nearly overwhelmed as he was with other trials, he would scarcely have attempted frequent trips into the interior. But in those years he took at least 10 evangelistic journeys, all of which were remarkable for their courage and endurance.

Endless waterways stretched north, south and west of Shanghai that gave access to the surrounding populous region. Flat-bottomed boats called junks were plentiful, and they provided shelter at night as well as transportation by day so that travelers were not dependent on Chinese inns. The boatman's family and "guests" made use of simple cooking arrangements for food. The beds were just wooden boards and the tiny windows were often on a level with the floor, but one could lie down or sit on one's bedding when it was not possible to stand upright. There were many inconveniences, but traveling in this way Taylor had access to people in city after city and town after town. Villages were never out of sight as the boat went slowly along.

Hudson Taylor was drawn to this huge number of people by compassion, the same way Jesus had been long ago. The same "must" was in his heart: "As long as it is day, we must do the work of him who sent me" (John 9:4); "I must preach the good news of the kingdom of God to the other towns also" (Luke 4:43); "I have other sheep that are not of this sheep pen. I must bring them also" (John 10:16). It was not enough to go to the highways and byways of Shanghai. Others were already doing that to some extent. His heart was burdened with a sense of responsibility for those beyond—those who never had heard the way of salvation, who never could hear unless the truth was brought to them by Christ-filled messengers. So nothing held him back, not the winter cold, summer heat or the war conditions, which endangered the lives of Europeans and could at any time cut him off from return to Shanghai.

No sooner was one journey completed than he would start preparations for another. After a period devoted chiefly to study, he spoke the language well enough to be understood in Mandarin as well as the local dialect. The trips that followed were so intensive that these 10 journeys were accomplished within 15 months. Before Dr. Parker arrived, Taylor made many excursions to places within 10 or 15 miles of Shanghai. During the first three months they were together, they distributed 1,800 New Testaments and Bible portions and more than 2,000 explanatory books and tracts. These were given with the utmost care, only to those who could read. Since the majority of those they met were illiterate and the crowds were constantly changing, each presentation required a great deal of explanation.

From January to March, Taylor took four journeys in spite of below freezing temperatures. These trips were followed by others in April, May, June, August and September. Because he was out among the crowds all day and sleeping in boats that had to be closed at night because of river thieves, there was little relief from the distressing heat. But nothing deterred the young evangelist.

These journeys were extremely dangerous, and when he traveled alone he was often very lonely. Far from other foreigners, moving among unfriendly crowds, he quietly carried out his mission. He found that his medical equipment was his most valuable tool in opening the way to people's hearts. His own heart, meanwhile, was entering more deeply into what it means to live and die "without Christ," and his passion and vision were growing. He would look from temple-crowned hilltops and the height of ancient pagodas down upon cities, towns and villages where the homes of millions of people were in sight—men, women and children who had never heard the only name "by which we must be saved" (Acts 4:12). God was moving in his heart in powerful ways.

In the midst of it all, the civil war had reached its climax, and Shanghai fell to the government forces. Hudson Taylor was traveling at the time with older missionaries west of Shanghai toward the Soochow Lake. They hadn't been gone long when they saw smoke from an immense fire rising from the top of a hill. A fire that big in that direction could mean only one thing—Shanghai was in flames! Their hearts raced in concern for their families back in the settlement. They left immediately to return to them, but their fears were confirmed by fleeing rebels who sought protection. Of course the missionaries could not comply, and the men were caught and beheaded before their eyes. Quickly moving on with increasing apprehension, they found terrible evidence of the catastrophe that had taken place. By God's grace, the settlement was as they had left it. Satiated with slaughter, the Imperialists were too exultant over their conquest to pay much attention to foreigners.

"Shanghai is now in peace," Hudson Taylor wrote, "but it is like the peace of death. Two thousand people at the very least have perished, and the tortures some of the victims have undergone cannot have been exceeded by the worst barbarities of the Inquisition. The city is little more than a mass of ruins, and many of the wretched objects who survive and are piteous to behold."

Still, the worst was over, and Hudson Taylor and his colleagues gave themselves to caring for the people, body and soul, while waiting for the reply of their committee to suggestions for more settled work. They longed to feel useful, and they had thought through their plans well and had spent much time in prayer over them. But the answer upon which their future seemed to depend took so long to arrive.

The heat of summer, meanwhile, was overpowering in their crowded quarters, and a brief visit to Ningpo opened a tempting possibility that brought with it tremendous changes. Feeling the need for a hospital to supplement their work, the missionaries in Ningpo extended an invitation to Dr. Parker to take up the challenge. While they were still waiting for the reply from their committee back in England, they received notice that the house they were sharing with another family would be needed shortly for members of the mission to which it belonged. Their fellow occupant was moving to a place of his own, but they had not been in a position to build, nor could they find rooms for rent anywhere in the settlement or Chinese city. Only one course seemed open to Hudson Taylor, especially when the long-expected answer came and was unfavorable. The committee was not prepared to spend money on building in the port areas. They wanted their workers to go to the interior, though where they were to live until that was feasible was not covered. Under these circumstances, Dr. and Mrs. Parker decided to go to Ningpo, and Hudson Taylor was left in uncertainty. With his friends gone, his home gone and no accommodations could be found even in the native city, how could he remain in Shanghai to carry on his work?

For a time he was very perplexed, but a new line of thought gradually emerged out of these difficulties. He had been searching unsuccessfully for any kind of place he could rent as a home base.

The rapid influx of a new population made the housing problem in Shanghai more acute than ever. If he could not get a home on shore, why not do what many Chinese were doing and move onto a boat to live on the water? This would fit in well with the project he already had in mind of adopting Chinese dress to be able to accomplish his work more easily. It all began to open up. He decided to take his few belongings to Ningpo when he escorted the Parkers there. When he returned he intended to identify himself completely with the people to whom his life was given.

But the step was not as simple as it seemed. Wearing Chinese dress in those days involved shaving the front part of the head and letting the hair grow long for the regulation queue. No missionary or other foreigner conformed to such a custom. For an occasional journey, a Chinese gown might be used over one's ordinary clothing, but to give up European dress and adopt the native costume altogether was quite another matter. Hudson Taylor realized that social ostracism would come with that kind of action. So for a time there was a struggle, though he was increasingly convinced of the wisdom of the step from a higher point of view.

He wanted access to the people. A recent 25-day journey in which he had penetrated 200 miles up the Yangtze River had assured him that it was possible to do more through itinerant evangelism than most believed. Of the 58 towns and cities he visited, 51 had never before been touched by messengers of the gospel. But the weariness and strain of the journey had been largely due to the fact that he was wearing European clothing, a most outlandish costume to those who had never seen it before! His message was continually lost as attention was captured by his appearance, which to his hearers was as undignified as it was comical. And after all, surely it mattered more to be suitably attired from the Chinese point of view—when it was the Chinese he wanted to win—rather than sacrifice their approval for that of the small foreign community in the ports. So he came to the decision at last, after much prayer and searching the word of God for guidance. When the Parkers were ready to leave for Ningpo, Hudson Taylor's Chinese outfit was ready, too. All that was left was to commit himself to the barber's transforming hands.

It was an August evening when he went down to the river to hire the junk that was to take the Parkers on the first stage of their journey. On the way, a Chinese stranger approached him and asked whether he was seeking a house for rent. Would a small one in the Chinese city do? This stranger told him that near the south gate there was a small house available that was still under construction. The owner had run short of money and did not know how to complete the work. If the house suited him, he would need no deposit, and he could probably have it for an advance of six months' rent.

Hudson Taylor followed his guide, as if in a dream, to the southern part of the city where he found a small, compact house, perfectly new and clean. It had two rooms upstairs, two on the ground floor, and a fifth across the courtyard for the helpers—just the thing he needed and in the location he would have chosen. He was elated to pay the money that night and secure the house for his own use. He had not been mistaken after all! His work in Shanghai was not finished. His prayers were being answered, and God was giving guidance for that which he had longed and waited.

That night he took the step which had an immense influence on the evangelization of inland China. When the barber had done his best, the young missionary darkened his remaining hair to match the long braid which, at first, was a fill-in for his own. In the morning he did his best to put on the loose, Chinese garments to appear for the first time in the gown and satin shoes of the "Teacher," or man of the scholarly class.

After that, everything opened up in a new way. On the return journey to Shanghai he was not even recognized as a foreigner until he began to preach or distribute books and see patients. Women and children came around much more freely, and the crowds were less noisy and excited. While he missed some of the prestige of being European, he found that his changed appearance gave him freedom that more than made up for the loss. He could finally move freely among the people. Their homes were open to him as never before, and it was possible to get opportunities for quiet discussions with those who seemed interested. Filled with thankfulness for these and other advantages, he wrote home about the dress he had adopted, "It is evidently to be one's chief help for the interior."

And it was "the interior" that his heart was set upon more and more. A few weeks in his new home at the south gate refreshed his soul.

"Dr. Parker is in Ningpo," he wrote early in October, "but I am not alone. I have such a sensible presence of God with me as I never before experienced, and such drawings to prayer and watchfulness as are very blessed and necessary."

Then, even though a little place of his own was welcome and he had many opportunities around him, Hudson Taylor set out again for the "regions beyond." His Christian teacher was left to look after the interested neighbors in Shanghai and other missionaries were doing fine, intensive work in the city as well. It might not seem fruitful—to go as far to the interior as possible, scattering the word of God—but it was following the Lord's teaching and example. Unless someone went to them, how would those farther inland ever hear at all?

Joy and sorrow strangely mingled in the days that followed. While his journey had gone very well, the outcome brought him into trouble. His destination was the island of Tsungming which had a population of more than a million without a single Protestant missionary. Hudson Taylor and Mr. Burdon had visited Tsungming the year before, but now a very different reception awaited him. At his first stop, the people simply would not let him leave. Dressed like them, he did not seem to be a foreigner. His medicine chest attracted them as much as his preaching, and when they learned that he would need an upstairs room because of the dampness of the area, they said, "Let him live in the temple, if no other upper story can be found."

But someone came forward with a house that included some sort of attic. Within three days of his arrival, Hudson Taylor found himself owning his first home in "inland China."

This was wonderful, and so was the response to his message. Neighbors dropped in to the meetings every day and the stream of visitors and patients seemed unceasing. While it stirred some opposition on the part of the medical workers, the work resulted in a group of earnest inquirers in just six weeks. One of these was a blacksmith named Chang and another a businessman in good standing, "whose heart the Lord opened." Kwei-hwa, the first to come to faith under Hudson Taylor's teaching, and another Christian helper worked closely with him, so that when Taylor had to return to Shanghai for supplies, the little group was still cared for.

Then the disappointment came which was as painful as it was unexpected. Unknown to him, there had been some conversations going in Tsungming. Some doctors and pharmacists had convinced a high official to relieve them of the presence of one whom they considered their rival, even though the young missionary accepted no payment for his medical work. Taylor was summoned to the British Consulate, and his plea to be allowed to remain on the island, where all seemed peaceful and friendly, was in vain. The Consul reminded him that the British treaty only provided for residence in the port cities and that if he attempted to settle elsewhere, he made himself liable to a fine of $500. He was ordered to give up his house, move his belongings to Shanghai and be careful not to break the rules in the future. This was difficult to accept when he knew that French priests were living on Tsungming, protected by a supplementary treaty which stipulated, as Hudson Taylor well knew, that immunities granted to other nations should also apply to the British. He might be able to appeal to a higher authority, but in the meantime he had to accept the Consul's decision.

He wrote a heartbroken letter home that evening. Those young inquirers—Chang, Sung and the others—what was to become of them? They were his own children in the faith, how could he leave them with no help and so little knowledge in the things of God? Yet the Lord had permitted it. The work was his. He would not fail them nor forsake them.

"My heart will be truly sorrowful when I can no longer join you in the meetings," said the blacksmith the last evening they were together.

"But you will worship in your own home," replied his friend. "Still shut your shop on Sunday, for God is here whether I am or not. Get someone to read for you and gather your neighbors in to hear the gospel."

"I know but very little," added Sung, "and when I read I by no means understand all the characters. My heart is grieved because you have to leave us; but I do thank God that he ever sent you to this place. My sins, once so heavy, are all laid on Jesus, and he daily gives me joy and peace."

Perplexed and disappointed, the young missionary could only wait upon God to show him what his future course should be.

"Pray for me, pray for me," he wrote to his parents at this time. "I need more grace, and live far below my privileges. Oh, to feel more as ... the Lord Jesus did when he said, 'I lay down my life for the sheep' (John 10:15). I do not want to be as a hireling who flees when the wolf is near, nor would I lightly run into danger when much may be accomplished in safety. I want to know the Lord's will and to have grace to do it, even if it results in expatriation. 'Now my heart is troubled, and what shall I say? ... Father, glorify your name' (John 12:27, 28). Pray for me, that I may be a follower of Christ not in word only, but in deed and in truth."

Completely unknown to this one with a troubled heart, there was someone stronger, with deeper faith than his own and more experienced in the things of God, who was facing the same problem. This man was also burdened for the perishing millions of inland China. He, too, had been testing the possibilities of itinerant evangelism and had found encouraging openings. He had failed, however, in his effort to reach Nanking and was confined to living on boats, slowly making his way back to the coast. William Burns, the preacher and evangelist whom God had used so powerfully throughout Scotland and Canada in the revival of 1839, was nearing Shanghai at the same time. God brought him into Hudson Taylor's life in his hour of need. It was not long before each recognized a kindred spirit, in spite of the many years between them. They drew together like Paul and Timothy, and God used those wintry days to build a friendship destined to mold not only Hudson Taylor's missionary life, but the character of the far-reaching enterprise that was to develop under his guidance.

Two boats now traveled together over the network of waterways leading inland from Shanghai. Both Taylor and Burns had a Chinese missionary with them as well as other helpers, and their daily worship on the boats grew into a full worship service. Burns had developed a pattern which his companion was glad to follow. They would choose a strategic center, and then they would stay two or three weeks in that place. Every morning they set out early with a definite plan, sometimes going together and sometimes separating to visit different parts of the area.

William Burns believed in beginning quietly on the outskirts of any city in which foreigners had rarely been seen and working his way by degrees to the more crowded central areas. They would give some days to preaching in the suburbs, gradually approaching the thronging streets and markets, until they could pass anywhere without causing a great stir. Then they would visit temples, schools and tea shops, returning regularly to the best places for preaching. At each meeting they would announce when they would be there again, so they had the satisfaction of seeing the same faces frequently. Those with higher interest were invited to the boats for further conversation.

As time went on, William Burns did not fail to notice that

Hudson Taylor, though so much younger and less experienced, had more attentive listeners and was even asked into private houses while he was asked to wait outside. The riffraff of the crowd always seemed to gather around the preacher in foreign dress, while those who wished to listen without being disturbed followed his less noticeable friend. Burns tells of the result in the following letter:

January 26, 1856

It is now 41 days since I left Shanghai on this last occasion. An excellent young English missionary, Mr. Taylor of the Chinese Evangelization Society, has been my companion ... and we have experienced much mercy, and on some occasions considerable help in our work.

I must once more tell the story I have had to tell more than once already, how four weeks ago, on the 29th of December, I put on Chinese dress which I am now wearing. Mr. Taylor had made this change a few months before, and I found that he was in consequence so much less incommoded in preaching, etc., by the crowd, that I concluded that it was my duty to follow his example. ...

We have a large, very large field of labor in this region, though it might be difficult in the meantime for one to establish himself in any particular place. The people listen with attention, but we need the power from on high to convince and convert. Is there any spirit of prayer on our behalf among God's people in Kilsyth? Or is there any effort to seek this spirit? How great the need is, and how great the arguments and motives for prayer in this case! The harvest here is indeed great, and the laborers are few and imperfectly fitted, without much grace, for such a work. And yet, grace can make a few feeble instruments the means of accomplishing great things—things greater even than we can conceive.

Prayer was the atmosphere of William Burns's life, and the word of

God was his daily food.

"He was mighty in the scriptures," his biographer records, "and his greatest power in preaching was the way in which he used 'the sword of the Spirit' upon men's consciences and hearts. ... Sometimes one might have thought, in listening to his solemn appeals, that one was hearing a new chapter in the Bible when first spoken by a living prophet. ... His whole life was literally a life of prayer, and his whole ministry a series of battles fought at the mercy-seat. ... In digging in the field of the word, he threw up now and then great nuggets which formed part of one's spiritual wealth ever after."

Cultured, cheerful, friendly and overflowing with wit, Burns was an ideal companion for Taylor. He loved sacred music, and he thoroughly enjoyed sharing anecdotes and recalling his experiences for the benefit of others. The friendship of this man, with all he was and had been, was the gift and blessing of God to Hudson Taylor at a crucial time. Under his influence Taylor grew and came to an understanding of spiritual values that made an impression on his whole life. William Burns was better to him than a college course with all its advantages, because he lived out before him, right there in China, the reality of all he most needed to be and know.

Burns and Taylor worked together for seven happy months, first in the Shanghai region, then in and around the city of Swatow. The call to this southern port had come quite unexpectedly, and they had the privilege of being the first missionaries in that difficult field. Without their Chinese dress, it would have been impossible to live right in the native city and to make friends with so many of their turbulent neighbors. At the end of four months they were able, through the blessing of God upon the medical work, to rent the entire building in which they had previously been allowed only a single room. It seemed that their initial difficulties had come to an end.

At Burns's request, Taylor consented to return to Shanghai to get the medical supplies that he had left there for safety. Hudson Taylor was reluctant to take the step—it was as if he sensed that they may be separated for a longer period of time. To leave Burns alone to face the worst heat of summer was just as distressing as breaking up the companionship which had meant so much in his life.

"Those happy months were an unspeakable joy and comfort to me," he recalled long after. "Never had I such a spiritual father as Mr. Burns; never had I known such holy, happy [conversation]. His love for the word was delightful, and his holy reverential life and constant communings with God made fellowship with him to satisfy the deep cravings of my heart."

The medical supplies were needed because Burns was interested in developing hospital work. So Hudson Taylor sailed for Shanghai where he found that his medical supplies had all been accidentally destroyed by fire. Before he could replace them, he received the distressing news that his beloved and honored friend had been arrested by the Chinese authorities and sent, under escort, on a 32-day journey to Canton. The shock was all the more painful because the two were forbidden to return to Swatow, and the path that had seemed so clear before them was lost in strange uncertainty.

If he had not endured this great and unexpected trial, however, Hudson Taylor might never have been led into the life work that was awaiting him, and he might never have known the love beyond all other human love which was to be his crowning joy and blessing.

CHAPTER 7

GOD'S WAY—"PERFECT"

We thank Thee, Lord, for pilgrim days
When desert springs were dry,
When first we knew what depths of need
Thy love could satisfy.
~ *Selected*

Over the political horizon, storm clouds had long been gathering, and the same mail that brought news of Mr. Burns's arrest told also of the outbreak of hostilities between England and China. Hudson Taylor was in Ningpo when he heard of the bombardment of Canton by the British fleet and the outbreak of the war which did not finally terminate until four years later. His first thought, naturally, was for Mr. Burns. What a mercy that he was no longer at Swatow, exposed to the rage of that hotheaded southern people!

"As you are aware," he wrote to his sister in November, "I have been detained in Ningpo by various circumstances, and a sufficient cause has at length appeared in the disturbances which have broken out in the south. The latest news we now have is that Canton has been bombarded for two days, a breach being made on the second, and that the British entered the city, the viceroy refusing to give any satisfaction. We are anxiously awaiting later and fuller accounts. ... I know not the merits of the present course of action ... and therefore refrain from writing my thoughts about it. But I would just refer to the goodness of God in removing Mr. Burns from Swatow in time. For if one may judge the feelings of the Cantonese in Swatow by what one sees here at present, it would go hard with anyone at their mercy."

So, already, the circumstance that had seemed a disaster was being recognized as among the "all things" that work together for good to them that love God. (See Rom. 8:28.) It was one of many hard lessons through which Hudson Taylor was learning to think of God as "The One Great Circumstance of Life" and of all lesser, external circumstances as the kindest, wisest and best, because they were either ordered or permitted by him. And it was not long before he came to see that through his detention in Ningpo, God was giving another remarkable evidence of his love and care. It was during this time and in this place that Taylor was brought into contact with the life that was so perfectly to complete his own.

In the southern section of the city, near an ancient pagoda, was Bridge Street, a quiet street that went between two lakes. Dr. Parker had opened a pharmacy a mile or two from his hospital, and this is where Hudson Taylor was glad to find a temporary home. (This little place became the first station of the China Inland Mission.)

Looking back upon those early days, Taylor wrote, "I have a distinct remembrance of tracing my initials on the snow which during the night had collected on my coverlet in the large, barn-like upper room now divided into four or five smaller ones, each of which is comfortably ceiled. The tiling of a Chinese house may keep off the rain, if it happens to be sound, but does not afford so good protection against snow, which will beat up through the crannies and crevices and find its way within. But however unfinished may have been its fittings, the little house was well adapted for work among the people, and there I thankfully settled, finding ample scope for service morning, noon and night."

The only other foreigners in that part of the city were Mr. and

Mrs. John Jones, also of the Chinese Evangelization Society, and Miss Mary Ann Aldersey, who, with two young helpers, was carrying on a remarkably successful school for girls, the first ever opened in China. She was assisted by the orphaned daughters of the Rev. Samuel Dyer, who had been one of the earliest missionaries to the Chinese. When the Jones family came to live not far from the school, the younger of the sisters, Maria Dyer, found many opportunities to help the busy mother. Miss Dyer was fluent in the language, so as often as possible, she and Mrs. Jones spent time visiting their neighbors. Even though she was young (not yet 20) and busy with her school responsibilities, this bright, gifted girl was a zealous evangelist. With her, missionary work was not merely teaching. It was leading people to Christ.

This was what caught Hudson Taylor's interest. It was inevitable that he would meet Miss Dyer from time to time in the home of his fellow workers, and he was attracted to her from the start. She was so frank and natural that they soon became good friends. Because she was like-minded in so many important ways, she began to fill a place in his heart never filled before.

Before Hudson Taylor could admit his affection for her even to himself, the friendship was interrupted by unexpected events which broke up the missionary community in Ningpo. They discovered a plot by the Cantonese to massacre all foreigners, and though it was stopped, the hatred that boiled throughout the district was so great that it seemed necessary to send families with children to the coast. Because Hudson Taylor was familiar with the Shanghai dialect, he was the obvious choice to escort the party. As hard as it was to leave, he knew he must serve in this way.

Miss Aldersey could not be persuaded to leave for a safer place. She was getting older and taking steps to retire and hand over management of the school to the American Presbyterian Mission. She wanted to avoid any unnecessary changes, and so, taking what precautions were possible, she encouraged the Dyer sisters to remain with her. Maria's sister had become engaged to Hudson Taylor's special friend, Mr. Burdon, which left Maria seeming more lonely and unprotected. It was very difficult to leave her in these circumstances. But Hudson Taylor had not shared his feelings with her and had no reason to believe that his presence would be any comfort to her.

Beside protecting his heart from being broken again, he was well aware of how little he had to offer the one he loved. His position with the Chinese Evangelization Society had become increasingly embarrassing. For some time he had known that the society was in debt and that his salary was paid from borrowed money.

He wrote, recalling the circumstances, "Personally, I had always avoided debt, though at times only by very careful economy. Now there was no difficulty in doing this, for my income was larger, but the society itself was in debt. The quarterly bills which I and others were instructed to draw were often met with borrowed money, and a correspondence commenced which terminated in the following year by my resigning from conscientious motives.

"To me it seemed that the teaching of God's word was unmistakably clear: 'Owe no man anything' [Rom. 13:8]. To borrow money implied to my mind a contradiction of scripture—a confession that God had withheld some good thing, and a determination to get for ourselves what he had not given. Could that which was wrong for one Christian be right for an association of Christians? Or could any amount of precedents make a wrong course justifiable? If the word taught me anything, it taught me to have no connection with debt. I could not think that God was poor, that he was short of resources, or unwilling to supply any want of whatever work was really his. It seemed to me that if there were a lack of funds to carry on work, then to that degree, in that special development, or at that time, it could not be the work of God. To satisfy my conscience I was therefore compelled to resign my connection with the society. ... It was a great satisfaction to me that my friend and colleague, Mr.

Jones, ... was led to take the same step, and we were both profoundly thankful that the separation took place without the least breach of friendly feeling on either side. ...

"The step we had taken was not a little trying to faith. I was not at all sure what God would have me do or whether he would so meet my need as to enable me to continue working as before. ... But God blessed and prospered me, and how glad and thankful I felt when the separation was really effected! I could look right up into my Father's face with a satisfied heart, ready by his grace to do the next thing as he might teach me, and feeling very sure of his loving care.

"And how blessedly he did lead me I can never, never tell. It was like a continuation of some of my earlier experiences at home. My faith was not untried; it often, often failed, and I was so sorry and ashamed of the failure to trust such a Father. But oh! I was learning to know him. I would not ever then have missed the trial. He became so near, so real, so intimate! The occasional difficulty about funds never came from an insufficient supply for personal needs, but in consequence of ministering to the wants of scores of the hungry and dying around us. And trials far more searching in other ways quite eclipsed these difficulties and being deeper brought forth in consequence richer fruits."

That winter famine refugees crowded to Shanghai from districts devastated by the Taiping Rebellion.* The poor whom they were feeding were in all stages of nakedness, sickness and starvation. They were living in low, arched tombs which they had broken open, or in any discarded building half in ruins. In addition to taking charge of one of the chapels of the London mission, Hudson Taylor was preaching daily in the city temple. He made time, however, to visit these refugees with Mr. Jones, ministering regularly to the sick and feeding many of the hungry.

Taylor was very busy, so it was not because of idleness that his thoughts turned constantly to Maria in Ningpo. He realized that God had given him a deep love, and that compelled him to soberly consider marriage and its implications.

Meanwhile, in Ningpo, God was also working in Maria, though there seemed to be more obstacles for her. Maria Dyer's nature was deep and tender. Lonely from childhood, she had grown up longing for a real heart-friend. She could hardly remember her father, and her mother had died when she was only 10 years old. Maria loved her missionary work, but it was a lonely post for a girl still in her teens, especially after her sister became engaged to be married.

And then, he had come—the young missionary who impressed her also shared her longings for holiness, usefulness and nearness to God. He was different from others—not more gifted or attractive, though he was bright and pleasing and full of quiet fun, but with something about him that made her feel rested and understood. He seemed to live in such a real world and to have such a real, great God. Though she hadn't spent much time with him, it was a comfort to know that he was near. He had only been in Ningpo for seven weeks, and she was surprised to find how much she missed him when he left to return to Swatow.

To her joy as well as surprise, the circumstances changed again and Hudson Taylor was back in Ningpo. Perhaps this is what helped her to realize her true feelings for him. In any case, she soon knew, and with her sweet, true nature did not try to hide it from her own heart and God.

Others in the missionary community often saw Taylor differently than she did. They disliked that he wore Chinese dress, and they did not approve of his making himself so entirely one with the people. But she loved his Chinese dress, or rather what it represented of his spirit. She understood and sympathized with his poverty and generous giving to the poor. Others could not comprehend his longing to reach the huge number of people in the interior who were without Christ, but that was the burden she carried in her own heart! She would choose that life, too, but as a woman it seemed impossible. So she prayed often for her friend, though she didn't show that to him.

Month after month went by while he was in Shanghai, and she had no idea that he was also praying about his feelings for her. And then, at last—a letter! He had written to declare his love for her and to ask if she would become engaged to him. She was filled with great and wonderful joy—the invitation wasn't a surprise, only a quiet outshining of what had long shone within. So she was not mistaken after all. They were for one another!

In her joy, she went to find her sister, and they celebrated together. The next thing was to tell Miss Aldersey, with hope that she would approve this engagement as she had her sister's. But when the older lady heard the story, she was indignant.

"Mr. Taylor! That young, poor, unconnected nobody. How dare he presume to think of such a thing? Of course the proposal must be refused at once, and that finally."

Maria tried in vain to explain how much he meant to her. That only made matters worse. And her kind Miss Aldersey, with the best intentions, proceeded to take the matter entirely into her own hands. The result was a letter written almost at Miss Aldersey's dictation, not only closing the whole affair, but requesting strongly that it might never be reopened.

Bewildered and heartbroken, the poor girl had no choice. She was too young and inexperienced, and far too shy in such matters, to withstand the decision of Miss Aldersey which was strongly reinforced by other friends. Shocked with grief and shame, she could only leave it in the hands of her heavenly Father. He knew, he understood. And in the long, lonely days that followed, even when her sister was won over to Miss Aldersey's position, she took refuge in the certainty that nothing, nothing was too hard for the Lord. "If he has to slay my Isaac," she assured herself again and again, "I know he can restore."

But when spring came again and Hudson Taylor and others were able to return from Shanghai, things became increasingly difficult.

Miss Aldersey, indignant at Hudson Taylor's reappearance, decided it was her responsibility to discourage him in every possible way. He could not attempt to see Miss Dyer after the letter she had written, and he had no clue about Maria's true attitude. Gifted and attractive, she had many seeking to court her who were openly encouraged. Chinese etiquette combined with well-meant diplomacy made it almost impossible for Hudson and Maria to meet. But both were praying. Though burdened by it all, both hearts were open to God, truly desiring his will. And he has wonderful ways of working!

It was an oppressively hot and humid afternoon in July, and in regular rotation it had come to Mrs. Jones' turn to be hostess for the prayer meeting. The usual number of ladies gathered, but it turned out to be easier to come to the meeting that day than to get away. For with scarcely any warning, a waterspout, sweeping up the tidal river, broke over Ningpo in a deluge followed by torrents of rain. Mr. Jones and Hudson Taylor, by this time a boarder in their family, were over at the pharmacy, delayed because of the flooded streets. Most of the visitors had left before they reached home, but a servant from the school was there who said that Miss Maria Dyer and a companion were still waiting for sedan chairs.

"Go into my study," said Mr. Jones, "and I will see what can be arranged."

It was not long before he returned, saying that the ladies were alone with Mrs. Jones, and they would be glad to see him. Hardly knowing what he did, the young man went upstairs and found himself meeting the one he passionately loved. True, there were others present—that was unavoidable because of Chinese conventions—but he hardly saw them. He hardly saw anything but her face. He had only meant to ask if he might write to her guardian in London—for permission. But now it all came out—he could not help it! And she? Well, there were only intimate friends with them, and it might be so long before they could meet again! Yes, she consented, and did much more than that. With a true woman's heart, she relieved his fears by letting him understand that he was just as dear to her as she could be to him. And then Hudson Taylor relieved the situation by saying, "Let us take it all to the Lord in prayer."

Four months was a long, long time to wait, especially when they knew that Miss Aldersey had written home to the distant relatives with her own point of view. What if the guardian in London was influenced by her strong letter? What if he refused his consent to the marriage? Both the young people were clear in their conviction that the blessing of God rested upon obedience to parents or those in parental authority.

"I have never known," Taylor wrote in later years, "disobedience to the definite command of a parent, even if that parent were mistaken, that was not followed by retribution. Conquer through the Lord. He can open any door. The responsibility is with the parent, in such a case, and it is a serious one. When the son or daughter can say in all sincerity, 'I am waiting for Thee, Lord, to open the way,' the matter is in his hands and he will take it up."

And God did take it up. Toward the end of November the long-awaited letters arrived, and they were favorable! After careful inquiry, the uncle in London was satisfied that Hudson Taylor was a missionary of unusual promise. The secretaries of the Chinese Evangelization Society and other sources had nothing but good to say of him. Deciding that any rumors he may have heard were simply that, he consented to his niece's engagement, requesting only that the marriage be delayed until she came of age. And that would be in just two months.

After that they were openly engaged. Those happy winter days made up for all that had gone before! The wedding was arranged for the week following January 16, the day that Maria turned 21.

"I never felt in better health or spirits in my life," wrote Hudson Taylor." ... I can scarcely realize, dear Mother, what has happened; that after all the agony and suspense we have suffered we are not only at liberty to meet and be much with each other, but that within a few days, D.V., we are to be married! God has been good to us. He has indeed answered our prayer and taken our part against the mighty. Oh, may we walk more closely with him and serve him more faithfully. I wish you knew my precious one. She is such a treasure! She is all that I desire."

And then, six weeks later: "Oh, to be married to the one you do love, and love most tenderly and devotedly ... that is bliss beyond the power of words to express or imagination conceive. There is no disappointment there. And every day as it shows more of the mind of your beloved, when you have such a treasure as mine, makes you only more proud, more happy [and] more humbly thankful to the Giver of all good for this best of earthly gifts."

CHAPTER 8

JOY OF HARVEST

Sheaves after sowing, sun after rain,
Sight after mystery, peace after pain.
~ Frances Ridley Havergal

Only two and a half years remained of Hudson Taylor's first period of service in China, but they were rich, full years. The little house on Bridge Street was now really home. Downstairs, the chapel and guest hall remained the same, and the Christians and visitors came and went freely, but upstairs one could hardly recognize the barn-like attic in the cheery little rooms whose curtained windows looked out on the narrow street in front and the canal behind. It was an increased blessing that the women and children could now be cared for equally with the men. Already well known in the neighborhood, Maria was even more welcome as she went visiting. The love shared between the Taylors affected all who saw them.

One of their warmest friends and helpers was Mr. Ni, an ex-Buddhist leader who was a cotton merchant in the city. Even though he had lived in Ningpo for a long time, he had never come in contact with the gospel. He was very devoted and spent much of his time and money in the service of "the gods." But his heart was not at rest, and the more he followed his religious observances, the more he found them to be empty.

Passing an open door on the street one evening, he noticed that something was going on. A bell rang and people assembled as if for a meeting. Learning that they were gathering to discuss religious matters, he went in as well. Mr. Ni was very concerned about sin and its penalties and was interested to know more of what happened as the soul went on its unknown way. A young foreigner in Chinese dress was preaching from his sacred classics. He was very comfortable speaking in the Ningpo dialect, and Mr. Ni could understand every word of the passage he read. But what could it mean?

"Just as Moses lifted up the snake in the desert, so the Son of Man must be lifted up, that everyone who believes in him may have eternal life. For God so loved the world that he gave his one and only Son, that whoever believes in him shall not perish but have eternal life. For God did not send his Son into the world to condemn the world, but to save the world through him" (John 3:14-17).

Saved, not condemned; a way to find everlasting life; a God who loved the world; a snake, no a "Son of Man" lifted up—what could it all be about? Ni's mind was racing! The story of the bronze snake in the wilderness, illustrating the divine remedy for sin and its deadly consequences; the life, death and resurrection of the Lord Jesus Christ; and what all of this meant for his own restless heart was brought home to him in the power of the Spirit.

But the meeting was coming to a close. The foreign teacher had finished speaking. With the instinct of one accustomed to lead in such situations, Ni rose in his place, and, looking round at the audience, said with simple directness, "I have long sought the truth, but without finding it. I have traveled far and near, but have never searched it out. In Confucianism, Buddhism [and] Taoism, I have found no rest. But I do find rest in what we have heard tonight. Henceforth, I am a believer in Jesus."

Mr. Ni became a passionate student of the Bible, and his growth in knowledge and grace was wonderful. Not long after his conversion, he received permission to address a meeting of the society over which he had formerly presided. Hudson Taylor accompanied him to the meeting and was deeply impressed by the clarity and fullness with which he shared the gospel. One of Ni's former followers was led to Christ through his testimony, and Ni began to know the joy of welcoming others into salvation.

One time, while talking with his missionary friend, Ni unexpectedly raised the question: "How long have you had the glad tidings in your country?"

"Some hundreds of years," was the reluctant reply.

"What! Hundreds of years? My father sought the truth," he continued sadly, "and died without finding it. Oh, why did you not come sooner?"

Hudson Taylor could never forget the pain of that moment, and it deepened his commitment and passion in seeking to bring Christ to those who might still be reached.

In those days Taylor and the others needed to be patient and not run before the Spirit of God when it came to engaging full-time helpers in the work. So far the young missionaries did not have regular Chinese associates. Mr. Ni was eagerly devoting all the time he could spare from his business, and so were Neng-kuei the basket-maker, Wang the farmer of Hosi, and Tsiu the teacher. But they and others were all busy doing their jobs during the day, though they drew to the mission house in the evening and spent much time there on Sundays.

It would have been easy to employ the Christian teacher in the school where Maria Taylor was giving many hours daily or to take on others at a modest salary to train them for positions of usefulness. But the missionaries realized that this would have proved a hindrance in the long run rather than a help. To pay young new believers, however sincere, for sharing the gospel—and to pay them with money from foreign sources—would inevitably weaken their influence if not their Christian character. The time might come when their call of God to such work, and his provision for that, would be evident to all. How was China ever to be evangelized except by the Chinese church? And how were these new believers going to know the joy of unpaid, voluntary service, out of love to the Lord Jesus Christ, unless the missionaries could be patient and wait for spiritual developments?

So Hudson Taylor and his colleagues led a full life while the young believers were growing up around them. His days were filled with medical work in addition to preaching on the streets and in the chapel, receiving visitors, managing correspondence and accounts and continuing with his evangelistic trips to the interior. But his priority of meeting with the Christians and inquirers daily remained his top priority.

It is not at all surprising that with such love and care, the new believers grew in grace and in knowledge of the things of God. Every evening the missionaries would be at their disposal. After the regular public meeting, they participated in three segments of studies. To begin with, Hudson Taylor delighted to unfold the spiritual teaching from the Old Testament. After a brief break, they read a chapter in Pilgrim's Progress or some other helpful book. And finally they talked over a passage from the New Testament and applied it to practical life. This was the order every night, and Sunday held special services for worship and for reaching outsiders in addition to times of study.

It cost the Christians significantly to close shops and stores on Sunday to be able to attend. Yet Hudson Taylor and his colleagues knew that strong churches can only be built on this basis. They determined to do their best to make the sacrifice worthwhile by filling these hours given to God with helpful and joyous times together. Between the regular services, Christians, visitors, patients, schoolchildren and servants were divided into classes and taught in a bright, personal way. This made Sunday a heavy day for the four missionaries, but with their own sacrifice they were better able to appreciate the sacrifices made by the new believers. Some believers had to walk long distances and go without food the greater part of the day, and others had to face persecution and personal loss. But most of them were willing to do whatever was necessary to have the Lord's day for worship. They had experienced the difference it made through the whole week.

God was growing the church and developing the missionaries, and more and more opportunities for service opened before them. The Treaty of Tientsin,* signed in the summer after Hudson and Maria's marriage, had opened the way to all the inland provinces. Foreigners now had the right to travel freely under the protection of passports, and now it was time to go and use the homes and mission posts that God had given them after much prayer.

"You will have heard before this all about the new treaty," Taylor wrote in November. "We may be losing some of our Ningpo missionaries ... who will go inland. And oh, will not the church at home awaken and send us out many more to publish the glad tidings?

"Many of us long to go—oh, how we long to go! But there are duties and ties that bind us that none but the Lord can unloose. May he give 'gifts' to many of the native Christians, qualifying them ... for the care of churches already formed, ... and thus set us free for pioneering work."

This was the burden on their hearts—to raise up, by the blessing of God, a church that would reproduce itself as well as support itself— and they could not set aside the little band of believers who still needed them as parents in the Lord. They had committed to love and pray for these souls, and to leave them now, even for the good of others, would have been to disregard the highest of all trusts, "parental" responsibility. The days that followed proved their conviction to be accurate.

For these Christians, Ni, Neng-kuei, Wang and the rest, were men whom God could use. Poor and unlearned as most of them were, they, too, were to become "fishers of men." At least six or seven of these early converts came to the help of their beloved leader in the formative years of the China Inland Mission. Without them, the new project, humanly speaking, could never have been realized. It would be difficult to overestimate all that grew out of the intensive work at Bridge Street during this time.

In the midst of all this great harvest, a great and unexpected sorrow called Hudson Taylor to new responsibilities. Over in the settlement, Dr. Parker had recently completed his new hospital. Situated near one of the city gates and overlooking the river, its spacious buildings attracted the notice of thousands daily. Everything about the place was adapted to the needs of the work built up over many years. But hearts were breaking in the doctor's home. This brave man who had overcome so many difficulties was mourning the loss of his wife, who had passed away after only a few hours' illness, leaving four young children. One of them was seriously ill, and the doctor realized that he must take them home to Scotland. But what about the hospital? The rooms were full of patients, and the pharmacy and treatment center was crowded day by day with a stream of people needing help. No other doctor was free to take his place, and yet to close down with the winter coming on seemed unthinkable. Though there were no funds to leave for the work—because it was supported from the proceeds of his private practice—perhaps his former colleague, Hudson Taylor, could at least keep the pharmacy and treatment center open?

"After waiting upon the Lord for guidance," Taylor recalled, "I felt constrained to undertake not only the [pharmacy and treatment center] but the hospital as well, relying solely on the faithfulness of a prayer—hearing God to furnish means for its support."

At times there were more than 50 in-patients in addition to a large number of people who used the services of the pharmacy and treatment center. Thirty beds were ordinarily allotted to free patients and those caring for them with about the same number available to opium smokers who paid their board while being cured of the habit. Because the treatment for the sick in the wards and the medical supplies needed for the out-patient department were supplied at no charge, the daily expenses were considerable. Hospital attendants were also required, and this needed support for them. The funds for the maintenance of all this had previously been supplied by the doctor's foreign practice, and with his departure this source of income ceased. But hadn't God said that whatever we ask in the name of the Lord Jesus shall be done (John 14:13)? And are we not told to seek first the kingdom of God—not means to advance it—and that "all these things" (Matt. 6:33) would be added to us? Such promises were surely sufficient.

It did not matter to the young missionaries that they had not looked for this situation, that none of their friends at home could have foreseen it or that months must go by before there could be any response to letters. They were looking only to the Lord for their support, and had he ever failed them? The secret of faith that is ready for emergencies is the quiet, practical dependence upon God day by day which makes him real to the believing heart.

"Eight days before entering upon the care of the Ningpo hospital," Taylor wrote, "I had not the remotest idea of ever doing so; still less could friends at home have foreseen the need."

But the Lord had anticipated it, as the events that followed fully proved.

When the assistants who remained after Dr. Parker had gone learned of the change in conditions, and that there were only funds in hand for the expenses of the current month, after which prayer would be the only resource, they very naturally decided to leave their positions, which opened the way for other workers. It was a change Dr. Parker had desired to make for quite some time, but he had not known how to get different helpers.

Hudson Taylor did know, and with a lightened heart he turned to the little circle that did not fail him. For to the Bridge Street Christians it seemed quite as natural to trust the Lord for temporal blessings as for spiritual. Did not the greater include the lesser; and wasn't God, as their "teacher" so often reminded them, a real Father, who never could forget his children's needs? So they came to the hospital, glad not only to strengthen the hands of their missionary friends, but to prove afresh the faithfulness of God to themselves and all concerned. Some worked in one way and some in another; some gave what time they could spare, and others gave their whole time without promise of wages, living only on the support they were provided. And all took the hospital and its concerns on their hearts in prayer.

A new atmosphere began to permeate the treatment center and wards. The patients could not account for it—not at first anyway—but they enjoyed the happy, homelike feeling, and the zest with which everything was carried on. The new attendants—Wang the grass-cutter and Wang the painter, Ni, Neng-kuei and others—seemed to possess the secret of perpetual happiness. Not only were they kind and considerate in the hospital work, but they gave all their spare time to telling of One who had transformed life for them and who, they said, was ready to receive all who came to him for rest. Then there were books, pictures and singing. Everything indeed seemed set to song! And the daily meetings in the chapel only made one long for more.

There are few secrets in China, and soon the patients knew all about the financial basis upon which the hospital was now run, and they were watching eagerly for the outcome. This was something more to think and talk about. As the money left by Dr. Parker was used up and Hudson Taylor's own supplies ran low, many conjectured as to what would happen next. Needless to say, Hudson Taylor gave himself to prayer at this time. It was, perhaps, a more open, and in that sense more crucial, test than any that had come to him previously, and he realized that the faith of many was at stake, as well as the continuance of the hospital work. But day after day went by without bringing the expected answer.

Finally one morning Kuei-hua, the cook, appeared with

serious news. The very last bag of rice had been opened, and it was disappearing rapidly.

"Then," replied Hudson Taylor, "the Lord's time for helping us must be close at hand."

And so it was. Even before they emptied that bag of rice, a letter reached the young missionary that was among the most remarkable he had ever received.

It was from Mr. William Berger, and it contained a check for 50 pounds, like others that had come before. Only, in this case, the letter went on to say that a heavy burden had come upon the writer, the burden of wealth to use for God. Mr. Berger's father had recently passed away, leaving him a considerable increase of fortune. The son did not wish to enlarge his personal expenditures. He had had enough before and was now praying to be guided as to the Lord's purpose in what had taken place. Could his friends in China help him? The draft enclosed was for immediate needs, and would they write fully, after praying over the matter, if there were ways in which they could profitably use more?

Fifty pounds! There it lay on the table, and his far-off friend, knowing nothing about that last bag of rice or the many needs of the hospital, actually asked if he might send them more. No wonder Hudson Taylor was overwhelmed with thankfulness and awe. Suppose he had held back from taking charge of the hospital on account of lack of means, or, rather, lack of faith? Lack of faith—with such promises and such a God?

The praise meeting held in the hospital chapel resounded with songs and shouts of joy. But the gathering had to be a short one— there were patients in the wards! And how those men and women who had known nothing all their lives but lifeless, empty heathenism listened to the celebration!

"Where is the idol that can do anything like that?" was the question upon many lips and hearts. "Have they ever delivered us in our troubles, or answered prayer like this?"

CHAPTER 9

HIDDEN YEARS

Oh, to save these! To perish for their saving;
Die for their life; be offered for them all.
~ Selected

All the busy, happy work began to weary the hospital staff. Within nine months, 16 patients from the hospital had been baptized while more than 30 others were candidates to join one or another of the Ningpo churches. But these challenging six years in China had left their mark, and Hudson Taylor's strength was failing rapidly.

"People are perishing, and God is so blessing the work," he wrote to his father. "But we are wearing down and must have help. ...

"Do you know of any earnest, devoted young men desirous of serving God in China, who, not wishing for more than their actual support, would be willing to come out and labor here? Oh, for four or five such helpers! They would probably begin to preach in Chinese in six months' time, and in answer to prayer the means for their support would be found."

"People are perishing, and God is so blessing the work"—it was the urgency of these facts that carried Hudson Taylor through serious illness and the painful parting when he returned home in 1860. It was the urgency of these facts that sustained him through the years that followed, when it seemed as though the doctors were right in thinking that he would never be strong enough to return to China. The great need he had seen and a deep sense of responsibility burned as a steady fire in his soul, and neither poor health, lack of encouragement or any other difficulty could lessen his sense of call to bring Christ to those perishing millions.

To be near his old hospital, Taylor settled in the east end of London, and as his health improved he was able to resume his medical studies. The Bible Society had agreed to publish a new edition of the Ningpo Testament, so he also began revising the roman script. For a time there was a good deal of correspondence with young men who were considering China as a field for life service, which resulted in the only one going out to join Mr. and Mrs. Jones in Ningpo. But gradually outside interest seemed to lessen, and the Taylors found themselves, with few friends, left only to prayer and patience. At 29 and 24 years old, it was not easy to be set aside, cut off from the work they loved and left in the backwater of that dreary street in a poor part of London. Yet, without those hidden years with all their growth and testing, how could the vision and enthusiasm of their youth have been matured for the leadership to which they would be called?

The five years in London were a time of growing intimacy with God and dependence upon him. Faith, faithfulness down to the smallest detail, devotion and self-sacrifice all led to unremitting labor. Taylor's patient and persevering prayer was wonderfully answered. But, even more, the deep, prolonged exercise of a soul that was following hard after God brought the gradual strengthening of this man called to walk by faith not by sight (2 Cor. 5:7), the unutterable confidence of a heart clinging to God alone.

Outwardly the days were filled with quiet, ordinary duties, enriched with trials and joys of many kinds. The little daughter who had brought such happiness in Ningpo now had three younger brothers. Home and children had to be cared for with very limited means, and faith was often tested as Hudson and Maria went on in the pathway of direct dependence upon God. The work in Ningpo needed provision and direction which involved a good deal of correspondence. The New Testament revision was a task that seemed to grow rather than diminish because Taylor had decided to add helpful marginal references. These had great value to the Ningpo Christians, and the labor of preparing them, which was not an easy task, brought great blessing to the young missionary who was spending hours every day in the word of God.

The amount of work he was enabled to accomplish was amazing. Every day Taylor noted in his journals the time given to his main task which shows the priority he gave to the translation work:

April 27, Revision seven hours (evening at Exeter Hall).

April 28, Revision nine and a half hours.

April 29, Revision 11 hours.

April 30, Revision five and a half hours (Baptist Missionary Society meetings).

May 1, Revision eight and a half hours (visitors till 10 p.m.).

May 2, Revision 13 hours.

May 3, Sunday at Bayswater: In the morning heard Mr. Lewis, from John 3:33; took the communion there in the afternoon. Evening, stayed at home and engaged in prayer about our Chinese work.

May 4, Revision four hours (correspondence and visitors).

May 5, Revision 11 and a half hours.

May 6, Revision seven hours (important interviews).

May 7, Revision nine and a half hours.

May 8, Revision 10 and a half hours.

May 9, Revision 13 hours.

May 10, Sunday: Morning, with Lae-djun on

Heb. 11, first part, a happy season. Wrote to James Meadows.

Afternoon, prayer with Maria about leaving this house, about

Meadows, Truelove, revision, etc. Wrote to Mr. Lord. Evening, heard Mr. Kennedy on Matt. 27:42—"He saved others, himself he cannot save." Oh, to be more like the meek, forbearing, loving Jesus! Lord, make me more like Thee.

The meetings referred to were a large part of Taylor's work at this time. He was doing all he could to persuade denominational boards and mission societies to engage in the evangelization of inland China. He shared with them the immense needs of the long-neglected field which had only recently been made accessible. When Taylor added his personal knowledge of certain parts of China to a careful study of the whole field, the result was overwhelming. Even though he found sympathetic listeners, it became evident that none of the boards was prepared to assume responsibility for such a large effort.

Taylor's heart was again stirred. What could he do to move others to grasp the urgency of bringing the gospel to China? Just at that time he had been requested by his friend and pastor, William Lewis, editor of the Baptist Magazine, to write a series of articles to awaken interest in the Ningpo mission. He had begun to prepare these articles, and one had already been published, when Mr. Lewis returned the manuscript of the second. The articles were too important and weighty, he felt, to be restricted to a denominational paper.

"Add to them," he urged, "let them cover the whole field and be published as an appeal for inland China."

This opportunity led Hudson Taylor to study in detail the spiritual needs of every part of China, including its outlying areas. While he was in Ningpo, the pressure of the needs surrounding him had been so great that he had been unable to give much thought to the still greater needs further inland. But now—facing the map on the wall of his study each day with the open Bible whose promises were gripping his soul—he was as near the vast provinces of inland China as the places in which he had labored near the coast. The more he learned the more he was drawn to pray that God would meet those needs.

A real crisis came, though, when prayer no longer brought relief in the burden, but instead it seemed to commit him more and more to the work from which he had been removed. He began to see in the light of the Bible that God could use him to answer his own prayers.

"I had a growing conviction," he wrote, "that God would have me seek from him the needed workers and go forth with them. But for a long time unbelief hindered my taking the first step. ...

"In the study of that divine word, I learned that to obtain successful workers, not elaborate appeals for help, but first earnest prayer to God to thrust forth laborers, and second the deepening of the spiritual life of the church, so that men should be unable to stay at home, were what was needed. I saw that the apostolic plan was not to raise ways and means, but to go and do the work, trusting his sure promise who has said, 'Seek ye first the kingdom of God and his righteousness, and all these things shall be added unto you' [Matt. 6:33]. ...

"But how inconsistent unbelief always is! I had no doubt but that if I prayed for fellow workers, in the name of the Lord Jesus Christ, they would be given. I had no doubt but that, in answer to such prayer, the means for our going forth would be provided, and that doors would be opened before us in unreached parts of the empire. But I had not then learned to trust God for keeping power and grace for myself, so no wonder I could not trust him to keep others who might be prepared to go with me. I feared that amid the dangers, difficulties and trials necessarily connected with such work, some comparatively inexperienced Christians might break down, and bitterly reproach me for encouraging them to undertake an enterprise for which they were unequal.

"Yet what was I to do? The sense of bloodguiltiness became more and more intense. Simply because I refused to ask for them, the laborers did not come forward, did not go out to China: and every day tens of thousands in that land were passing into Christless graves! Perishing China so filled my heart and mind that there was no rest by day and little sleep by night, till health gave way."

The years in London had done their work. God had formed an instrument that he could use, and the prayers going up from that little home in East London were to receive a speedy though unexpected answer.

CHAPTER 10

A MAN SET ASIDE FOR GOD

Nothing before, nothing behind:
The steps of faith
Fall on the seeming void, and find
The rock beneath.
~ John Greenleaf Whittier

Summer had come again, and the streets were hot and dusty in East London. Seeing that Hudson Taylor was not looking well, an old friend invited him down to the coast to spend a few days at Brighton. Maria, who was concerned about his health, was glad to see him go, though she understood only in part the experiences through which he was passing. He could not fully show, even to her, the exercise of his soul that was becoming unbearable.

So Taylor was alone on the sands of Brighton beach that Sunday morning when he met the crisis of his life. He had gone to church with others, but the sight of multitudes rejoicing in the blessings of salvation was more than he could bear. "I have other sheep that are not of this sheep pen"—the lost and perishing in China, for whose souls no man cared—"I must bring them also" (John 10:16). The tones of the master's voice and the love in the master's face pleaded silently.

Taylor knew that God was speaking. He knew that if he yielded to his will and prayed under his guidance, God would give evangelists for inland China. He had no anxiety about their support. He who called and sent them would not fail to give them daily bread. But what if they should fail? Hudson Taylor was not facing an unknown situation. He was familiar with conditions in China, the real temptations they would meet, and the real enemy entrenched on his own ground. What if the fellow workers could not manage under the weight and they laid the blame on him?

"It was just a bringing in of self through unbelief; the devil getting one to feel," he recalled, "that while prayer and faith would bring one into the fix, one would have to get out of it as best one might. And I did not see that the power that would give the men and the means would be sufficient to keep them also, even in the far interior of China."

Meanwhile, a million a month were dying in that great, waiting land—dying without God. This burned into Taylor's soul. He had to make a decision and he knew it, because he could no longer endure the conflict. It was comparatively easy to pray for workers, but would he, could he, accept the burden of leadership?

"In great spiritual agony, I wandered out on the sands alone. And there the Lord conquered my unbelief, and I surrendered myself to God for this service. I told him that all the responsibility as to the issues and consequences must rest with him; that as his servant it was mine to obey and to follow him, his to direct, care for and guide me and those who might labor with me. Need I say that at once peace flowed into my burdened heart?

"Then and there I asked him for 24 fellow workers, two for each of the 11 provinces which were without a missionary and two for Mongolia; and writing the petition on the margin of the Bible I had with me, I turned homeward with a heart enjoying rest such as it had been a stranger to for months, and with an assurance that the Lord would bless his own work and that I should share in the blessing. ...

"The conflict ended, all was peace and joy. I felt as if I could fly up the hill to Mr. Pearce's house. And how I did sleep that night! My dear wife thought that Brighton had done wonders for me, and so it had."

CHAPTER 11

A MAN SENT FROM GOD

Thou on the Lord rely,
So safe shalt thou go on;
Fix on his work thy steadfast eye,
So shall thy work be done.
~ Paul Gerhardt

Happy is the man called to go forward in any pathway of faith who has in his life-companion only sympathy and help. For seven and a half years—perfect years as concerned their married life—Hudson Taylor had known no disappointment in the one he loved, and she did not fail him now. Frail in health and only 28 years old, Maria Taylor's hands were full with the care of four young children; yet from the moment she learned of her husband's call to the great, seemingly impossible task of the evangelization of inland China, she became in a new way his comfort and inspiration. She wrote for him, her faith strengthened his own, her prayers undergirded the whole work, and her practical experience and loving heart made her the "mother of the mission."

Soon the larger house at Coborn Street into which they had moved began to fill up with candidates for China. The parlors that had seemed so spacious could scarcely accommodate the friends who gathered for the Saturday prayer meeting. The $50 (all he had) with which Taylor had opened a bank account in the name of "The China Inland Mission" grew into hundreds through the voluntary, unasked gifts of those who desired to have a part in the work. It seemed that in no time a plan began to form for the first party to head out to China.

Picture the sitting room at Number 30 Coborn Street on a Sunday—the only day when Taylor could find time for quiet writing. At the table Maria is seated, pen in hand, while he paces to and fro, absorbed in the subject on their hearts. The articles Mr. Lewis suggested had taken on new meaning. There was not only an urgent need to make known, but a new departure, a definite effort to meet that need in dependence upon God. The booklet China's Spiritual Need and Claims came into being as they prayed and wrote, wrote and prayed; and perhaps no book of the time proved more effective in moving the hearts of the people of God. Until the secrets of all hearts are revealed, we will not know how many were sent to China as edition after edition was published, how many were drawn into sympathy with missionary work all over the world, or how it strengthened faith and quickened prayer and devotion. Every sentence was steeped in prayer, and every sentence seemed to live with the power of God.

The booklet created many opportunities and with that, many new friends and supporters from all over the country. It had to be reprinted within three weeks of publication, and it drew responses such as the following from the late Lord Radstock: "I have read your pamphlet and have been greatly stirred by it. I trust you may be enabled by the Holy Spirit to speak words which will thrust forth many laborers into the vineyards. Dear Brother, enlarge your desires! Ask for 100 laborers, and the Lord will give them to you."

Taylor did not ask for 100, but the prayer recorded in his Bible was for 24 as the first objective. He was not elated at the turn of events as the success only added to his sense of responsibility. Taylor was a man burdened with a God-given message, and he moved from place to place that memorable winter, awakening other hearts to the same God-consciousness.

It was a new thing, in those days, to talk about faith as a sufficient financial basis for missionary work at the other end of the world. "Faith missions" were unheard of, as the only organizations that existed were the regular denominational boards. But Hudson Taylor, even though he was young, had learned to know God and his faithfulness in a very real way. He had seen him calm storms, stop the actions of would-be murderers and pacify enraged men in answer to prayer. He had seen God heal sickness and revive the dying when all hope of recovery seemed gone. For more than eight years God had proved his faithfulness in supplying the needs of his family and work in answer to prayer, unforeseen as many of those needs had been. Hudson Taylor was eager to call others to trust God and his unfailing faithfulness.

"We have to do with one," he reminded his hearers, "who is Lord of all power and might, whose arm is not shortened that it cannot save, nor his ear heavy that it cannot hear; with one whose unchanging word directs us to ask and receive that our joy may be full, to open our mouths wide, that he may fill them. And we do well to remember that this gracious God, who has condescended to place his almighty power at the command of believing prayer looks not lightly on the blood-guiltiness of those who neglect to avail themselves of it for the benefit of the perishing. ...

"To those who have never been called to prove the faithfulness of the covenant-keeping God ... it might seem a hazardous experiment to send 24 European evangelists to a distant heathen land 'with only God to look to'; but in one whose privilege it has been, through many years, to put that God to the test—at home and abroad, by land and sea, in sickness and in health, in dangers, necessities, and at the gates of death—such apprehensions would be wholly inexcusable."

The work they were undertaking was far too great to be limited to any one denomination. The fact that the mission offered no salaries was in itself enough to deter all but those whose experience made them sure of God.

"We had to consider," Taylor continued, "whether it would not be possible for members of various denominations to work together on simple, evangelistic lines, without friction as to conscientious differences of opinion. Prayerfully concluding that it would, we decided to invite the cooperation of fellow believers, irrespective of denominational views, who fully held the inspiration of God's word and were willing to prove their faith by going to inland China with only the guarantee they carried in their Bibles.

"That word said, 'But seek ye first the kingdom of God, and his righteousness; and all these things (food and raiment) shall be added unto you' [Matt. 6:33]. If anyone did not believe that God spoke the truth, it would be better for him not to go to China to propagate the faith; if he did believe it, surely the promise sufficed. Again, we have the assurance, 'no good thing will he withhold from them that walk uprightly' [Ps. 84:11]. If anyone did not mean to walk uprightly, he had better stay at home; if he did mean to walk uprightly, he had all he needed in the shape of a guarantee fund. God owns all the gold and silver in the world, and the cattle on thousand hills. We need not be vegetarians!

"We might indeed have had a guarantee fund if we had wished it; but we felt that it was unnecessary and would do harm. Money wrongly placed and money given from wrong motives are both greatly to be dreaded. We can afford to have as little as the Lord chooses to give, but we cannot afford to have unconsecrated money, or to have money placed in the wrong position. Far better to have no money, even to buy bread with. There are plenty of ravens in China, and the Lord could send them again with bread and flesh. ... He sustained 3 million Israelites in the wilderness for 40 years. We do not expect him to send 3 million missionaries to China, but if he did he would have ample means to sustain them all.

"Let us see that we keep God before our eyes; that we walk in his ways and seek to please and glorify him in everything, great and small. Depend upon it, God's work, done in God's way, will never lack God's supplies."

One thing greatly concerned Taylor and that was that the new enterprise should not deflect men or means from previously existing agencies. "Robbing Peter to pay Paul," in this sense, would be no advantage to the work of God. In response, Taylor created standards for the mission that would take this into consideration. It was part of the plan to open the way for workers who might not be accepted by other missions or whose preparation had not included university training, and no one was to be asked to join the China Inland Mission. If the Lord of the harvest wanted them in that particular field, he would put it into their hearts to offer. In the same way, there were to be no appeals for money. If the mission could be sustained in answer to prayer, without subscription lists or solicitation of any kind for funds, it might grow up among the older societies without danger of diverting gifts from their normal channels. It would also be helpful because it gave a practical illustration of the underlying principle that God alone is sufficient for God's own work.

They were content with little in the way of managing the organization. God provided wonderfully for the home side of the work in William and Mary Berger of Saint Hill Manor. They were nearly as passionate about the work as the Taylors. They prayed for it, lived for it with equal devotion and turned their beautiful home into a center for all the interests of the mission.

"When I decided to go forward," Taylor said of this relationship, "Mr. Berger undertook to represent us at home. The thing grew up gradually. We were much drawn together. The China Inland Mission received its name in his drawing room. Neither of us asked or appointed the other—it just was so."

Taylor and Berger reviewed essential, spiritual principles with the candidates and sought to ensure that they clearly understood the basis of the mission. In Mr. Berger's presence they agreed to a few simple arrangements in writing, and that was all that was required for joining.

"We came out as God's children at God's command," was Taylor's simple statement, "to do God's work, depending on him for supplies; to wear native dress and to go inland. I was to be the leader in China. ... There was no question as to who was to determine points at issue."

In the same way, Mr. Berger was responsible at home. He would correspond with candidates, receive and forward contributions, publish an Occasional Paper with audited accounts, send out suitable reinforcements as funds permitted and keep clear of debt. This last was a cardinal principle with all concerned.

"It is really just as easy," as Taylor pointed out, "for God to give beforehand, and he much prefers to do so. He is too wise to allow his purposes to be frustrated for lack of a little money; but money obtained in unspiritual ways is sure to hinder blessing."

There were problems, many of them, that only experience could solve, and Mr. Berger's practical illustration often came to mind. He was the head of a prosperous starch manufacturing business. He knew that like the trees on his estate, a living thing will grow.

"You must wait for a tree to grow," he said, "before there can be much in the way of branches. First you have only a slender stem, with a few leaves or shoots. Then little twigs appear. Ultimately, these may become great limbs, all but separate trees. But it takes time and patience. If there is life, it will develop after its own order."

God clearly answered many prayers as the first party made their preparations for sailing. He had provided so abundantly that in the first Occasional Paper they made an announcement that the whole sum needed for passage and outfits was already in hand. All involved with the mission understood that behind these experiences was prayer. They had gathered during the noon hour every day in Taylor's home as well as for the weekly gathering there and at Saint Hill, and, in addition, they held special days for prayer and fasting.

They enjoyed a very close and happy walk with God.

Human nothingness, divine sufficiency—the one just as real as the other—was the atmosphere of those last days at Coborn Street. Friends could not come and go without feeling it. Among suitcases and the flurry of final details, the last prayer meetings were held with people crowding the rooms and staircase and sitting on anything they could find. The map still hung on the wall and the open Bible was on the table.

"Our great desire and aim," Taylor had written of the new mission, "is to plant the standard of the cross in the 11 provinces of China hitherto unoccupied, and in Chinese Tartary."

Those who saw only the difficulties called it a foolhardy business.

"A superhuman task," sighed others who wished them well. And even many of their friends were anxious.

"You will be forgotten," was the concern of some. "With no committee or organization before the public, you will be lost sight of in that distant land. Claims are many nowadays. Before long you may find yourselves without even the [necessities] of life!"

"I am taking my children with me," was the quiet answer, "and I notice it is not difficult to remember that they need breakfast in the morning, dinner at midday and supper at night. Indeed, I could not forget them if I tried. And I find it impossible to think that our heavenly Father is less tender and mindful of his children than I, a poor earthly father, am of mine. No, he will not forget us!"

And through all the years since then, with all they have brought, that confidence has been amply justified.

CHAPTER 12

SPIRITUAL URGENCY

Men die in darkness at your side,
Without a hope to cheer the tomb;
Take up the torch and wave it wide,
The torch that lights time's thickest gloom.
~ *Horatius Bonar*

The leaders and many of the first workers of the new mission possessed a clearly evident sustaining power. There was an urgency of spirit that characterized them—a great, twofold urgency that carried them through every kind of difficulty and trial. There was the urgency of love to the Lord Jesus Christ that made them glory in their privilege of knowing him in the fellowship of his sufferings (Phil. 3:10) in a new and deeper way, and there was in them the urgency of his constraining love for the souls of the perishing by whom they were surrounded.

The first China Inland Mission party of 16 missionaries with the Taylors and their four young children set sail on a four-month voyage on the Lammermuir, a relatively small sailing ship of less than 800 tons. They had bathed the entire journey in prayer, not only for safety but for a crew whom God would bless through his faithful servants. They spent the first day getting things in order in their cabins, but by the second day the work began. Taylor taught the morning Chinese lessons, and Maria taught the one in the afternoon. There were times when all the students were down with seasickness, and the teachers had to do duty as steward and stewardess. But they were good sailors, and the younger people soon found their sea legs. They were all quite young, with their leader at 34 being by far the senior of them all.

Character was tested in the close quarters of that little sailing ship, and it was easy for the crew to see how far these passengers lived up to their profession. Needless to say, they were watched closely both when they were working and in their hours of relaxation. Doing all they could to make the voyage pleasant for the ship's company, the missionaries prayed and waited. Then the sailors themselves asked for meetings, and a work of God began which resulted in the conversion of a large majority of the crew. The written record of these events makes it very evident that the pioneers of the mission were living for nothing less than to win people to Christ. They were not faultless—there were failures that hindered blessing. But these were not taken as a matter of course. They were deplored and confessed with a sincerity which restored fellowship in the Lord.

It seemed, however, that since the great adversary was unable to discourage their passion and effectiveness in witness, that he was determined to send them, ship and all, to the bottom. It was nothing short of a miracle that they ever reached their destination. All the way up the China Sea they were hard-pressed by powerful storms. For 15 days the stress of one typhoon after another battered them, until they were almost a wreck.

"The appearance of things was now truly terrific," Taylor wrote after 12 days of this experience. "... Rolling fearfully, the masts and yards hanging down were tearing our only sail ... and battering like a ram against the mainyard. The deck from forecastle to poop was one scarcely broken sea. The roar of the water, the clanging of chains, the beating of the dangling masts and yards, the sharp smack of the torn sails made it almost impossible to hear any orders that might be given."

For three days after that the danger only increased, as the ship was taking on water fast. Fires were all out and cooking was impossible. For a time no drinking water was obtainable, and the women as well as the men worked at the pumps. But through it all, prayer was so wonderfully answered that no lives were lost and no one was seriously injured. Kept in the peace which passes understanding, even Maria, who was anxious for her children, was given strength. She wrote, "To enter into Habakkuk's experience as never before—'yet I will rejoice in the Lord, I will be joyful in God my Savior'" (Hab. 3:18).

Just as God was with them through the storms at sea, he was also present with them as they set out from Shanghai, all in Chinese dress, to seek a home inland. Traveling by houseboats, the women and children could be sheltered from curious crowds as they passed city after city while efforts were being made to find places for some of the young men to settle. But only disappointment awaited them. Again and again when it seemed they had succeeded, negotiations fell through and they had to move on all together toward Hangchow. Two or three missionary families were already living there, and it could have meant serious risk to them as well as to the new missionaries if the arrival of such a large party stirred up opposition. Yet, what were they to do? It was already deep into fall and the nights on the water were bitterly cold. Several of them were more or less ill, and the houseboat owners were eager to go home for the winter. Hudson Taylor felt the full weight of his responsibilities when he left the boats in a quiet place outside the city and went ahead to seek the accommodations they needed so urgently.

Maria was also feeling the burden as with quiet, confident faith she gathered the younger missionaries for prayer, telling them of the comfort that had come to her through the Psalm in her regular reading that morning: "Who will bring me to the fortified city? Who will lead me to Edom? Is it not you, O God. ... Give us aid against the enemy, for the help of man is worthless" (Ps. 60:9-11). They read it now together, and the prayer that followed changed an hour of painful suspense into one of sweet fellowship.

Could it be Hudson Taylor's voice that stirred the houseboat people outside? Could he be back so soon? "Before they call I will answer; while they are still speaking I will hear" (Is. 65:24). All was well! A home was ready, waiting for them. One of the Hangchow missionaries was absent for a week and had left word that his house, comfortably furnished, was at the disposal of Taylor's group. The house was situated on a quiet street, and they could reach it with the boats without being seen. That very night the weary, thankful travelers were at rest in the great city.

Within the next few days, in spite of all the usual difficulties, Taylor found a place of their own—a large rambling house which had once been an official's residence. This home was easy to adapt to their needs, and while they were only part owners, they were able to begin missionary work within their own home without attracting too much attention. One does not need many words for a loving heart to overflow, and Miss Faulding, the youngest of the party, was already able to make herself understood by the area women.

"We have been getting the house a little more comfortable," Miss Faulding wrote in the middle of December, "though there is plenty still to be done. Mr. Taylor and the young men have contrived paper ceilings fixed on wooden frames, which keep out some of the cold air—for the upstairs rooms have roofs such as you find in chapels at home. They also have papered some of the partitions between the rooms. Of course we are as yet in confusion, but we are getting on, and I hope shall be settled some day.

"The lodgers are to leave next week. They occupy principally the ground floor. ... I am so glad for them to have been here, for many have come to Chinese prayers and listened attentively. We could not have visited out of doors yet ... but I read and talked with those women every day and they seem to like it. One woman I have great hope of.

"Before Christmas there were attentive audiences of 50 or 60 at the Sunday services, and Mr. Taylor had made at least one evangelistic journey. In the neighboring city of Siaoshan, he and James Meadows had found excellent opportunities for preaching the gospel and had been enabled to rent a small house, with a view to settling out some of the new arrivals as soon as possible. His letters to Mr. Berger show the spirit in which they were facing their great task.

"You will be glad to learn that facilities for sending letters by native post and for transmitting money ... to the interior are very good. I do not think there will be any difficulty in remitting money to any province in the empire which will not be easily overcome. In the same way, letters from the most distant parts can be sent to the ports. Such communication is slow and may prove rather expensive, but it is tolerably sure. Thus we see the way opening before us for work in the interior.

"It is pretty cold weather [Dec. 4] to be living in a house without any ceilings and with very few walls and windows. There is a deficiency in the wall of my own bedroom six feet by nine, closed in with a sheet, so that ventilation is decidedly free. But we heed these things very little. Around us are poor, dark heathen—large cities without any missionary, populous towns without any missionary, villages without number, all without the means of grace. I do not envy the state of mind that would forget these, or leave them to perish, for fear of a little discomfort. May God make us faithful to him and to our work."

Meanwhile Taylor's hands were more than full in Hangchow. With the Chinese New Year, patients crowded to the clinic, as many as 200 in a day, and an equal number attended the Sunday services. Early in 1867 when the first reinforcements arrived from home, Taylor was too busy to see them until hours later. He was standing on a table at the time, preaching to a crowd of patients in the courtyard, and he could only call out a hearty welcome as James Meadows led the group in. The new arrivals accepted this easily, and it was not long before John McCarthy was at Taylor's side, soon to become his chief helper in the medical work. Those were days when, amid external hardships, Taylor's fellow workers had the opportunity of working closely with the leader they loved.

"I think of him as I ever knew him," John McCarthy wrote from western China 38 years later, "kind, loving, thoughtful of everyone but himself, a blessing wherever he went and a strength and comfort to all with whom he came in contact ... a constant example of all that a missionary ought to be."

Yet there were some, even in those early days, who became critical of all around them. The negative spirit that had caused trouble on the voyage was still apparent, and Maria suffered just as much as her husband through the damaging remarks that were made. They were so anxious to conquer the trouble by love and patience, however, that it wasn't until months later that she mentioned the matter in writing to Mary Berger. It was in answer to inquiries from Saint Hill that she wrote at length:

"Do pray for us very much, for we do so need God's preserving grace at the present time. We have come to fight Satan in his very strongholds, and he will not let us alone. What folly were ours, were we here in our own strength! But greater is he that is for us than all that are against us. ... I should be very sorry to see discord sown among the sisters of our party, and this is one of the evils I am fearing now. ... What turn the N—matter will take I cannot think. One thing I know: 'the hope of Israel' will not forsake us. One is almost tempted to ask, 'Why was N—permitted to come out?' Perhaps it was that our mission might be thoroughly established on right bases early in its history."

Sorrows of another kind were permitted to test faith and endurance as the summer wore on, but all the while souls were being saved and the church grew to more than 1,500 members. When the first baptisms came in May, Maria wrote again to Mrs. Berger: "Perhaps the dear Lord sees that we need sorrows to keep us from being elated at the rich blessing he is giving in our work."

But she could not have anticipated the overwhelming personal sorrow the hot season was to bring.

Their little daughter, Gracie, the sweetest and brightest of all their children, was born in Ningpo and was by this time almost eight years old. Full of love to the Lord Jesus and to the people around them, she was a great helper in the work as well as with her younger brothers, to whom she was all a sister could be. But with the long hot days, Gracie began to droop, and though the children were taken to the hills, nothing could save her life.

Beside his dying child in the old, ruined temple, Hudson Taylor faced the situation for himself and those he loved best.

"It was no vain nor unintelligent act," he wrote to Mr. Berger, "when, knowing this land, its people and climate, I laid my wife and children with myself on the altar for this service. And he whom we so unworthily, yet in simplicity and godly sincerity, are and have been seeking to serve—and with some measure of success—he has not left us now."

To his mother, Taylor wrote more freely.

"Our dear little Gracie! How we miss her sweet voice in the morning, one of the first sounds to greet us when we woke, and through the day and at eventide! As I take the walks I used to take with her tripping figure at my side, the thought comes anew like a throb of agony, 'Is it possible that I shall nevermore feel the pressure of that little hand ... nevermore see the sparkle of those bright eyes?' And yet she is not lost. I would not have her back again. I am thankful she was taken, rather than any of the others, though she was the sunshine of our lives. ...

"I think I never saw anything so perfect, so beautiful as the remains of that dear child. The long, silken eyelashes under the finely arched brows; the nose, so delicately chiseled; the mouth, small and sweetly expressive; the purity of the white features ... all are deeply impressed on heart and memory. Then her sweet little Chinese jacket, and the little hands folded on her bosom, holding a single flower—oh, it was passing fair, and so hard to close forever from our sight!

"Pray for us. At times I seem almost overwhelmed with the internal and external trials connected with our work. But he has said, 'I will not fail thee nor forsake thee' [Josh. 1:5], and 'my strength is made perfect in weakness' [2 Cor. 12:9]. So be it."

In the sorrow of their loss the Taylors gave themselves anew to the task of reaching inland China with the gospel. Before the close of the year, all the governing cities in Chekiang had been visited. Nanking, in the neighboring province had been reached by a missionary, and the members of the mission were working in centers as far as 24 days' journey apart. Wang Lae-djun pastored the well-established church in Hangchow, and as spring came again, it was possible for the leaders of the mission to get involved in other places.

In those days opening a new station in China required risking one's own life. Riots were so common that they seemed almost part of the proceedings, and it was natural for Hudson Taylor to say to one candidate who had lost a limb and could only walk with the help of a crutch, "But what would you do in China if a riot broke out and you had to run away?"

"I had not considered running away," was the quiet answer. "I thought that 'the lame' were to 'take the prey'" [Is. 33:23].

And this he did, in actual fact, when the time came and he had the privilege of living amid the troubles through which the gospel came to Wenchow.

"Why don't you run away?" yelled the rioters who were robbing him of everything and had taken even his crutches.

"Run away!" he replied with a smile. "How can a man run with only one leg, I should like to know?"

Disarmed by his courage and friendliness, the rioters stopped and calm came again.

In the same spirit of confidence, George Duncan, the tall, quiet Highlander, became the first resident missionary in Nanking.

When he could get no other lodging in the city, he was content to live in the drum tower where he shared an open loft with the rats and the deep-toned bell, spending his days amid the crowds in the street and tea shop. When his supply of money was running low, his Chinese cook and only companion came to ask what they should do—leaving the city and the little place they had rented would probably mean no possibility of return.

"Do?" questioned the missionary. "Why, we shall 'trust in the Lord, and do good.' So shall we 'dwell in the land' and verily we shall be fed" [Ps. 37:3].

Days went on, and Taylor was unable to get the needed finances to Nanking by native banks. Finally, in his anxiety for Duncan, he sent a brother-missionary, William Rudland, by boat with money to relieve the situation. By this time the cook's savings, willingly given to the work, were all used up, and between them they didn't even have a dollar left. But Duncan had gone out to his preaching as usual, saying to his anxious companion, "Let us just 'trust in the Lord and do good.' His promise is still the same, 'So shalt thou dwell in the land, and verily thou shalt be fed'."

That evening Rudland understood why the water in the Grand Canal had run so low that he had to finish his journey over land by foot. It brought him to Nanking several days earlier than would have been possible by boat. When he reached the house, he found the cupboards just as empty as Duncan's bank account. Tramping the endless streets, Duncan had preached all day and was returning tired and hungry when, to his surprise, he saw his Chinese helper running to meet him.

"Oh, sir," he cried breathlessly, "it's all right! It's all right! Mr. Rudland—the money—a good supper!"

"Did I not tell you this morning," Duncan replied, laying a kindly hand on his shoulder, "that it is always 'all right' to trust in the living God?"

* * * * *

But Hudson Taylor was not content with just getting the young men out into pioneering work. There were no dangers or hardships which he and Maria themselves were not ready to face, and the inward, spiritual passion was at least as strong in their hearts as in the hearts of others in the mission. It was not easy to leave Hangchow after 16 months of settled life and work. The church already had 50 baptized believers, and many of the inquirers were full of promise. But with Wang Lae-djun as pastor, assisted by John McCarthy, and with Jenny Faulding caring for the women, the good work would go on. There were lonely pioneers needing help, and teeming cities, towns and villages entirely without the gospel. Though it meant breaking up their home and taking the children to live on boats for a time, they set out in the spring, ready to join Duncan at Nanking or to stay in any place that might open to them along the way.

After two months of boat life, the travelers were able to settle in the city of Yangchow. They had spent three weeks with Henry Cordon, a member of the mission who was just beginning his work in the far-famed city of Soochow, before arriving at Chinkiang at the junction of the Grand Canal with the mighty Yangtze River. Impressed with the strategic importance of this place, Taylor quickly began negotiations for a property to have a mission there. Eventually they obtained the property, but because they realized that the negotiations were likely to take many weeks, they continued their journey across the Yangtze and a few miles up the northern section of the Grand Canal where they reached Yangchow, the famous city of which Marco Polo had once been governor. Within its turreted walls lived 360,000 people without any witness for Christ.

"Were it not that you yourselves are old travelers," Maria wrote to Mrs. Berger, "I should think it impossible for you to realize our feelings last Monday week, when we exchanged the discomfort of a boat into every room of which the heavy rain had been leaking, for a suite of apartments in a first-rate Chinese hotel—such a place as my husband, who has seen a good deal of Chinese travelers' accommodations, never before met with—and that hotel, too, inside the city of Yangchow."

At the beginning a friendly innkeeper and crowds of interested visitors were very encouraging. After the governor gave a favorable proclamation, the family was able to obtain a house and move into it in the middle of July. The heat was already trying, and they were hoping for quieter days in August, but the rush of patients and visitors continued. A foreign family in the city was a huge attraction, especially since Hudson Taylor proved to be a skillful physician. Maria's pleasing Chinese speech and manners attracted the women, and just as in Hangchow, hearts were opening to the gospel.

But the enemy was busy. Such an advance into his territory would not go unchallenged. The scholars of the city held a meeting and decided to stir up trouble. Anonymous posters began to appear all over the city, attributing the most revolting crimes to foreigners, especially those whose business it was to propagate "the religion of Jesus." Before long, the missionaries realized that a change was coming over the attitude of the people. Friendly visitors were replaced by crowds of the lowest rabble, and a fresh set of posters added fuel to the flame. Rioting was averted again and again through patience and kindness—Taylor, answering questions and keeping the crowds in order, hardly dared to leave the entrance to the premises for several days.

When the storm seemed to have spent itself, the additional gift of the arrival of the Rudlands and George Duncan filled the household with gratefulness. The intense heat of August was broken by torrential rains which scattered the crowds. But the relief was short-lived. Two foreigners from Chinkiang caused quite a stir when they came up to visit Yangchow wearing undisguised foreign clothing, not the Chinese dress adopted by the missionaries. This opportunity was too good to be lost. The scholars were busy again, and no sooner had the visitors left with the impression that all was quiet, than reports began to be circulated that children were missing in all directions. The people believed that at least 24 had fallen prey to the inhuman foreigners.

The troublemakers were crying out to the people: "Courage—avenge our wrongs! Attack! Destroy! Much loot shall be ours!"

* * * * *

Forty-eight hours later, in a boat nearing Chinkiang, wounded, suffering but undismayed, the group of missionaries was thanking God for his marvelous protection in the storm of the riot that had almost overwhelmed them.

"Our God has brought us through," Maria wrote as they traveled. "May it be to live henceforth more fully to his praise and glory. We have had another typhoon, so to speak, not as prolonged as the literal one, nearly two years ago, but at least equally dangerous to our lives and more terrible while it lasted. I believe God will bring his own glory out of this experience, and I hope it will tend to the furtherance of the gospel. ... Yours in a present Savior. ..."

"A present Savior"—how little could the rioters have understood the secret of such calmness and strength! Awed by something they did not understand, the raging mob had been restrained from the worst deeds of violence. Death, though imminent, had been averted again and again, and both Hudson Taylor, exposed to all the fury of the crowds on his way to seek the help of local authorities, and those he had had to leave, who faced the attackers and a fire consuming their home, were all protected by the unseen hand of God.

But they were hours of anguish—anguish for the mother as she sheltered the children and women of the party in an upper room from which they were driven at last by fire; anguish for the father, detained at a distance, hearing from the governor's palace the yells of the rioters bent on destruction. Outwardly as calm as if there were no danger, Maria Taylor faced those terrible scenes, more than once saving lives by her presence of mind and perfect command of the language, her heart meanwhile torn with anxiety for the loved one they might never see again.

Before the Yangchow house was repaired and they were permitted to return, the Taylor's endured long and trying negotiations. At the homecoming reception, it was with thankfulness that Hudson Taylor was able to write: "The results of this case will in all probability greatly facilitate work in the interior." But it was the family life and friendly spirit of the missionaries that gradually disarmed suspicion. Actions speak louder than words, and neighbors had something to think over when the children were brought back after all that had happened. When it was clear that Maria had not hesitated to return, the whole neighborhood joined in the desire for peace and quietness.

"In this again," she wrote to her beloved friend, Mrs. Berger, "God has given me the desire of my heart. For I felt that if safety to my infant permitted it, I would rather it were born in this city, in this house, in this very room than in any other place—your own beautiful home not excepted, in which I have been so tenderly cared for, and the comforts and luxuries of which I know so well how to appreciate."

The arrival of a fourth son and the speedy recovery of all who had been injured in the riot was a great testimony to onlookers. These things led to the innkeeper who had first received them in the city and two others who had risked much to befriend them during the riot to become believers in Christ and candidates for baptism. It seemed the storm had passed.

CHAPTER 13

DAYS OF DARKNESS

Against me earth and hell combine;
But on my side is Power Divine;
Jesus is all, and he is mine.
~ W. T. Matson

At home in England, Mr. Berger was facing an even worse storm that winter than had broken over the little mission in China. The Yangchow riot had stirred up criticism in Parliament and throughout the country to an extent that hardly seemed credible. Based upon misunderstandings, the public press was bitter in its attack on missionaries who had brought the country to the verge of war with China, it was stated, demanding the protection of British gunboats in their campaign to induce the Chinese to change their religion "at the mouth of the cannon and point of the bayonet." Needless to say, Hudson Taylor and his colleagues had given little, if any, ground for such criticism. Their case had been taken up by the consular authorities in a way that the missionaries neither expected nor desired. Acting under instructions from the foreign office, its representatives were quick to make the most of the opportunity to press for treaty rights, but before the reasonable demands of the British ambassador were complied with, a change of government in England complicated the situation. Maria Taylor, writing to relieve her husband, gave the full details to the Bergers.

"As to the harsh judgings of the world," she concluded, "or the more painful misunderstandings of Christian brethren, we generally feel that the best plan is to go on with our work and leave it to God to vindicate our cause. But it is right that you should know intimately how we have acted and why. I would suggest, however, that it would be undesirable to print the fact that Mr. [Sir Walter Henry] Medhurst, the consul general, and through him Sir Rutherford Alcock, took the matter up without application from us. The new Ministry at home censures those out here for the policy which the late Ministry enjoined upon them. It would be ungenerous and ungrateful were we to render their position still more difficult by throwing all the onus, so to speak, on them."

There was nothing they could do but to weather the storm, which continued long after life in Yangchow had become peaceful again, with prayer and patience. Four months later, Mr. Berger wrote from Saint Hill.

"The Yangchow matter is before the House of Lords. ... You can scarcely imagine what an effect it is producing in the country. Thank God I can say, 'None of these things move me' [Acts 20:24]. I believe he has called us to this work, and it is not for us to run away from it or allow difficulties to overcome us. ... Be of good courage; the battle is the Lord's."

It was doubly painful that, during such a time of crisis, certain members of the mission who had caused trouble from the very first continued to voice their dissatisfaction, and Taylor determined that it was time to request their resignations. Their representation of the issues of concern added to the misunderstandings at home, and in spite of Mr. Berger's wise, strong leadership, many friends were alienated from the work. This, combined with the criticisms in the public press, affected income in a serious way. The leaders of the mission were facing many large trials all at the same time.

"Pray for us," Taylor wrote soon after the riot. "We need much grace. You cannot conceive the daily calls there are for patience, for forbearance, for tact in dealing with the many difficulties and misunderstandings that arise among so many persons of different nationality, language and temperament. Pray the Lord ever to give me the single eye, the clear judgment, the wisdom and gentleness, the patient spirit, the unwavering purpose, the unshaken faith, the Christlike love needed for the efficient discharge of my duties. And ask him to send us sufficient means and suitable helpers for the great work which we have as yet barely commenced."

In the midst of it all the pioneer evangelism to which the mission was called continued on. Even before Yangchow matters were settled, Taylor had taken an important journey up the Grand Canal to a city from which he hoped to reach the northern provinces, and James Meadows had left his work in Ningpo to others so that he could lead an advance into the first inland province westward from Chinkiang—Anhwei Province. This province had 20 million among whom there wasn't a single Protestant missionary.

But instead of the increase of men and means for which they were praying, there was a marked drop in the funds reaching them from home. Although they couldn't yet see it, God was already preparing provision for the situation.

A penniless man in England—literally with no more financial resources than the birds of the air or lilies of the field—was already supporting a family of some 2,000 orphaned children (later increased to 4,000) through prayer and faith. Without a cent of endowment, without an appeal of any kind for help, without even letting their wants be known to anyone but the Father in heaven, on whose promise he relied, George Müller was proving the faithfulness of God in a way that had long stimulated Hudson Taylor's faith and that of many others. But this man of God in Bristol had such a large heart that he could not be content without participating directly in missionary work in the darker places of the earth. He prayed for funds to donate to the preaching of the gospel in many lands, including China, and he had the joy of being the Lord's channel of help in many difficult situations. It seemed as if the Lord had his ear in quite a special way and could use him in ministries that others overlooked.

No sooner had the Yangchow riot taken place, for example, and long before the news could have reached England, it was laid on Müller's heart to send financial help to the China Inland Mission (CIM). He was already contributing, but within a day or two of the riot, he wrote to Mr. Berger asking for the names of other members of the mission whom he might add to his list for ministry and prayer. Mr. Berger sent him six names from which to choose, and his choice was to take them all.

And then, a year later, when the shortage of funds was being most seriously felt in China, Müller wrote again, increasing his gifts. While that letter was on its way, Hudson Taylor, in sending out a December payment, wrote to one of the workers:

"Over 1,000 pounds less has been contributed during the first half of this (financial) year than last year. I do not keep a cook now. I find it cheaper to have cooked food brought in from an eating-house at a dollar a head per month. ... Let us pray in faith for funds, that we may not have to diminish our work."

To diminish his comforts seemed of small account, but "to diminish our work"—well, thank God, that was something he never had to do! Before the year closed, George Müller's letter was in his hands.

"My dear Brother," it read, "the work of the Lord in China is more and more laid on my heart, and hence I have been longing and praying to be able to assist it more and more with means, as well as with prayer. Of late I have especially had a desire to help all the dear brethren and sisters with you with pecuniary means. This I desired especially that they might see that I was interested in them personally. This my desire the Lord has now fulfilled."

The 11 checks enclosed were for all the members of the mission to whom Müller had not previously been ministering. Writing by the same mail, Mr. Berger said: "Mr. Müller, after due consideration, has requested the names of all the brethren and sisters connected with the CIM, as he thinks it well to send help as he is able to each one, unless we know of anything to hinder. ... Surely the Lord knew that our funds were sinking, and thus put it into the heart of his honored servant to help."

It was not only the money, but it was also the prayerful sympathy of such a man that made his gifts such a wonderful encouragement.

"My chief object," he wrote in his letter to the missionaries, "is to tell you that I love you in the Lord; that I feel deeply interested about the Lord's work in China, and that I pray daily for you.

"I thought it might be a little encouragement to you in your difficulties, trials, hardships and disappointments to hear of one more who feels for you and who remembers you before the Lord. But were it otherwise, had you even no one to care for you—or did you at least seem to be in a position as if no one cared for you—you will always have the Lord to be with you. Remember Paul's case at Rome. (See 2 Tim. 4:16-18.)

"On him then reckon, to him look, on him depend: and be assured that if you walk with him, look to him and expect help from him, he will never fail you. An older brother, who has known the Lord for 44 years, who writes this, says for your encouragement that he has never failed him. In the greatest difficulties, in the heaviest trials, in the deepest poverty and necessities, he has never failed me; but because I was enabled by his grace to trust in him, he has always appeared for my help. I delight in speaking well of his name."

Taylor desperately needed that encouragement, because, strange as it may seem, the trouble that followed the Yangchow riot had been light compared with the trials he carried within himself. Perhaps it was partly stress of outward circumstances that had hindered spiritual joy and rest; and yet, no amount of trial ever before clouded his rejoicing in the Lord.

"It doesn't matter, really, how great the pressure is," he used to say; "it only matters where the pressure lies. See that it never comes between you and the Lord—then, the greater the pressure, the more it presses you to his breast."

But at that time he had not learned the secret that later made his life so radiant, and he spent many hours struggling with depression, almost despair. He shared his weight in a letter to his mother:

"I have often asked you to remember me in prayer, and when I have done so there has been much need of it. That need has never been greater than at present. Envied by some, despised by many, hated by others, often blamed for things I never heard of or had nothing to do with, an innovator on what have become established rules of missionary practice, an opponent of mighty systems of heathen error and superstition, working without precedent in many respects and with few experienced helpers, often sick in body as well as perplexed in mind and embarrassed by circumstances—had not the Lord been specially gracious to me, had not my mind been sustained by the conviction that the work is his and that he is with me in what it is no empty figure to call 'the thick of the conflict,' I must have fainted or broken down. But the battle is the Lord's, and he will conquer. We may fail—do fail continually—but he never fails. Still, I need your prayers more than ever.

"My position becomes continually more and more responsible, and my need greater of special grace to fill it. But I have continually to mourn that I follow at such a distance and learn so slowly to imitate my precious Master.

"I cannot tell you how I am buffeted sometimes by temptation. I never knew how bad a heart I have. Yet I do know that I love God and love his work, and desire to serve him only and in all things. And I value above all else that precious Savior in whom alone I can be accepted. Often I am tempted to think that one so full of sin cannot be a child of God at all. But I try to throw it back, and rejoice all the more in the preciousness of Jesus and in the riches of the grace that has made us 'accepted in the beloved' [Eph. 1:6]. Beloved he is of God; beloved he ought to be of us. But oh, how short I fall here again! May God help me to love him more and serve him better. Do pray for me. Pray that the Lord will keep me from sin, will sanctify me wholly, will use me more largely in his service."

Despite the great faith that had brought him around the world to China and through tremendous pressures and losses, Hudson Taylor had never before felt so inadequate and in need of God's powerful intervention in his life.

CHAPTER 14

THE EXCHANGED LIFE

Yes, in me, in me he dwelleth—
I in him and he in me!
And my empty soul he filleth
Now and through eternity.
~ Horatius Bonar

Six months after his letter was written, a junk northbound on the Grand Canal was carrying a passenger whose heart overflowed with a great, newfound joy. Charles Judd was expecting the return of his friend and leader to Yangchow, but he was hardly prepared for the transformation which had taken place in the one he knew so well. Scarcely waiting for greetings, Hudson Taylor plunged into his story. In characteristic fashion—his hands behind his back—he walked up and down the room exclaiming, "Oh, Mr. Judd, God has made me a new man! God has made me a new man!"

The experience that had come in answer to prayer was wonderful, yet it was so simple. It was just as it was long ago, "I was blind but now I see!" (John 9:25).

Amid a pile of letters waiting for Taylor in Chinkiang was one from John McCarthy, written in the old home in Hangchow. The glory of a great sunrise was upon him—the inward light whose dawning makes all things new. He longed to tell Hudson Taylor about it because he knew something of the soul struggle through which his friend was passing. He tried to put it into words.

"I do wish I could have a talk with you now," he wrote, "about the way of holiness. At the time you were speaking to me about it, it was the subject of all others occupying my thoughts, not from anything I had read ... so much as from a consciousness of failure—a constant falling short of that which I felt should be aimed at; an unrest; a perpetual striving to find some way by which one might continually enjoy that communion, that fellowship, at times so real but more often so visionary, so far off! ...

"Do you know, I now think that this striving, longing, hoping for better days to come is not the true way to holiness, happiness or usefulness. It is better, no doubt, far better than being satisfied with poor attainments, but not the best way after all. I have been struck with a passage from a book ... entitled Christ is All. It says, 'The Lord Jesus received is holiness begun; the Lord Jesus cherished is holiness advancing; the Lord Jesus counted upon as never absent would be holiness complete. ... He is most holy who has most of Christ within, and joys most fully in the finished work. It is defective faith which clogs the feet and causes many a fall.'

"This last sentence, I think I now fully endorse. To let my loving Savior work in me his will, my sanctification, is what I would live for by his grace. Abiding, not striving nor struggling; looking off unto him; trusting him for present power; ... resting in the love of an almighty Savior, in the joy of a complete salvation, 'from all sin'— this is not new, and yet 'tis new to me. I feel as though the dawning of a glorious day had risen upon me. I hail it with trembling, yet with trust. I seem to have got to the edge only, but of a boundless sea; to have sipped only, but of that which fully satisfies. Christ literally all seems to me, now, the power, the only power for service, the only ground for unchanging joy. ...

"How then to have our faith increased? Only by thinking of all that Jesus is and all he is for us: his life, his death, his work, he himself as revealed to us in the word, to be the subject of our constant thoughts. Not a striving to have faith ... but a looking off to the faithful one seems all we need; a resting in the loved one entirely, for time and for eternity."

"As I read, I saw it all," Taylor wrote. "I looked to Jesus, and when I saw—oh, how joy flowed!"

"He was a joyous man now," Judd recorded, "a bright happy Christian. He had been a toiling, burdened one before, with latterly not much rest of soul. It was resting in Jesus now, and letting him do the work—which makes all the difference. Whenever he spoke in meetings after that, a new power seemed to flow from him, and in the practical things of life a new peace possessed him. Troubles did not worry him as before. He cast everything on God in a new way and gave more time to prayer. Instead of working late at night, he began to go to bed earlier, rising at 5 a.m. to give time to Bible study and prayer (often two hours) before the work of the day began."

It was the exchanged life that had come to him. Six months earlier he had written, "I have continually to mourn that I follow at such a distance and learn so slowly to imitate my precious master." He no longer thought of imitation. It was in blessed reality "Christ lives in me" (Gal. 2:20). The difference in him was immense—instead of bondage, liberty; instead of failure, quiet victories within; instead of fear and weakness, a restful sense of sufficiency in Christ. The deliverance was so great, that from that time onward Taylor sought to make this precious secret plain to whomever he could, beginning with his friends and family. It was to his sister, Mrs. Amelia Broomhall, whose burdens with a family of 10 children were very real and pressing.

"So many thanks for your dear, long letter. ... I do not think you have written me such a letter since our return to China. I know it is with you as with me—you cannot—not will not. Mind and body will not bear more than a certain amount of strain, or do more than a certain amount of work.

"As to work—mine was never so plentiful, so responsible or so difficult, but the weight and strain are all gone. The last month or more has been, perhaps, the happiest of my life, and I long to tell you a little of what the Lord has done for my soul. I do not know how far I may be able to make myself intelligible about it, for there is nothing new or strange or wonderful—and yet, all is new! ...

"Perhaps I may make myself more clear if I go back a little. Well, dearie, my mind has been greatly exercised for six or eight months past, feeling the need personally and for our mission of more holiness, life, power in our souls. But personal need stood first and was the greatest. I felt the ingratitude, the danger, the sin of not living nearer to God. I prayed, agonized, fasted, strove, made resolutions, read the word more diligently, sought more time for meditation—but all without avail. Every day, almost every hour, the consciousness of sin oppressed me.

"I knew that if only I could abide in Christ all would be well, but I could not. I would begin the day with prayer, determined not to take my eye off him for a moment, but pressure of duties, sometimes very trying, and constant interruptions apt to be so wearing, caused me to forget him. Then one's nerves get so fretted in this climate that temptations to irritability, hard thoughts and sometimes unkind words are all the more difficult to control. Each day brought its register of sin and failure, of lack of power. To will was indeed 'present with me,' but how to perform I found not.

"Then came the question, is there no rescue? Must it be thus to the end—constant conflict, and too often defeat? How could I preach with sincerity that, to those who receive Jesus, 'to them gave he power to become the sons of God' (John 1:12; i.e., godlike) when it was not so in my own experience? Instead of growing stronger, I seemed to be getting weaker and to have less power against sin; and no wonder, for faith and even hope were getting low. I hated myself, I hated my sin, yet gained no strength against it. I felt I was a child of God. His Spirit in my heart would cry, in spite of all, 'Abba, Father.' But to rise to my privileges as a child, I was utterly powerless.

"I thought that holiness, practical holiness, was to be gradually attained by a diligent use of the means of grace. There was nothing I so much desired as holiness, nothing I so much needed; but far from in any measure attaining it, the more I strove after it, the more it eluded my grasp, until hope itself almost died out, and I began to think that—perhaps to make heaven the sweeter—God would not give it down here. I do not think that I was striving to attain it in my own strength. I knew I was powerless. I told the Lord so, and asked him to give me help and strength. Sometimes I almost believed that he would keep and uphold me; but on looking back in the evening—alas! There was but sin and failure to confess and mourn before God.

"I would not give you the impression that this was the only experience of those long, weary months. It was a too frequent state of soul, and that towards which I was tending, which almost ended in despair. And yet, never did Christ seem more precious; a Savior who could and would save such a sinner! ... And sometimes there were seasons not only of peace but of joy in the Lord; but they were transitory, and at best there was a sad lack of power. Oh, how good the Lord has been in bringing this conflict to an end!

"All the time I felt assured that there was in Christ all I needed, but the practical question was—how to get it out. He was rich truly, but I was poor; he was strong, but I weak. I knew full well that there was in the root, the stem, abundant fatness, but how to get it into my puny little branch was the question. As gradually light dawned, I saw that faith was the only requisite—was the hand to lay hold of his fullness and make it mine. But I had not this faith.

"I strove for faith, but it would not come; I tried to exercise it, but in vain. Seeing more and more the wondrous supply of grace laid up in Jesus, the fullness of our precious Savior, my guilt and helplessness seemed to increase. Sins committed appeared but as trifles compared with the sin of unbelief which was their cause, which could not or would not take God at his word, but rather made him a liar! Unbelief was, I felt, the damning sin of the world; yet I indulged in it. I prayed for faith, but it came not. What was I to do?

"When my agony of soul was at its height, a sentence in a letter from dear McCarthy was used to remove the scales from my eyes, and the Spirit of God revealed to me the truth of our oneness with Jesus as I had never known it before. McCarthy, who had been much exercised by the same sense of failure but saw the light before I did, wrote (I quote from memory):

"'But how to get faith strengthened? Not by striving after faith, but by resting on the faithful one.'

"As I read, I saw it all! 'If we believe not, he abideth faithful' [2 Tim. 2:13]. I looked to Jesus and saw (and when I saw, oh, how joy flowed!) that he had said, 'I will never leave thee' [Heb. 13:5].

"'Ah, there is rest!' I thought. 'I have striven in vain to rest in him. I'll strive no more. For has not he promised to abide with me—never to leave me, never to fail me?' And, dearie, he never will.

"Nor was this all he showed me, nor one half. As I thought of the vine and the branches, what light the blessed Spirit poured direct into my soul! How great seemed my mistake in wishing to get the sap, the fullness out of him! I saw not only that Jesus will never leave me, but that I am a member of his body, of his flesh and of his bones. The vine is not the root merely, but all—root, stem, branches, twigs, leaves, flowers, fruit. And Jesus is not that alone—he is soil and sunshine, air and showers, and 10 thousand times more than we have ever dreamed, wished for or needed. Oh, the joy of seeing this truth! I do pray that the eyes of your understanding too may be enlightened, that you may know and enjoy the riches freely given us in Christ.

"Oh, my dear sister, it is a wonderful thing to be really one with a risen and exalted Savior, to be a member of Christ! Think what it involves. Can Christ be rich and I poor? Can your right hand be rich and your left poor? Or your head be well fed while your body starves? Again, think of its bearing on prayer. Could a bank clerk say to a customer, 'It was only your hand, not you, that wrote that check'; or 'I cannot pay this sum to your hand, but only to yourself'? No more can your prayers or mine be discredited if offered in the name of Jesus (i.e., not for the sake of Jesus merely, but on the ground that we are his, his members) so long as we keep within the limits of Christ's credit—a tolerably wide limit! If we ask for anything unscriptural, or not in accordance with the will of God, Christ himself could not do that. But 'if we ask any thing according to his will' [1 John 5:14] ... we know that we have the petitions that we desired of him.

"The sweetest part, if one may speak of one part being sweeter than another, is the rest which full identification with Christ brings. I am no longer anxious about anything, as I realize this; for he, I know, is able to carry out his will, and his will is mine. It makes no matter where he places me, or how. That is rather for him to consider than for me; for in the easiest position he must give me his grace, and in the most difficult his grace is sufficient. It little matters to my servant whether I send him to buy a few cash worth of things, or the most expensive articles. In either case he looks to me for the money and brings me his purchases. So, if God should place me in serious perplexity, must he not give much guidance; in positions of great difficulty, much grace; in circumstances of great pressure and trial, much strength? No fear that his resources will prove unequal to the emergency! And his resources are mine, for he is mine, and is with me and dwells in me.

"And since Christ has thus dwelt in my heart by faith, how happy I have been! I wish I could tell you about it, instead of writing. I am no better than before. In a sense, I do not wish to be, nor am I striving to be. But I am dead and buried with Christ—ay, and risen too!— And now Christ lives in me, and 'the life that I now live in the flesh, I live by the faith of the Son of God, who loved me and gave himself for me' [Gal. 2:20]. ...

"And now I must close. I have not said half I would, nor as I would, had I more time. May God give you to lay hold on these blessed truths. Do not let us continue to say, in effect, 'Who shall ascend into heaven?' (that is, to bring Christ down from above) [Rom. 10:6]. In other words, do not let us consider him as far off, when God has made us one with him, members of his very body. Nor should we look upon this experience, these truths, as for the few. They are the birthright of every child of God, and no one can dispense with them without dishonoring our Lord. The only power for deliverance from sin or for true service is Christ."

It was all so simple and practical, even the busy mother found this when she too entered into this rest of faith.

"But are you always conscious of abiding in Christ?" Hudson Taylor was asked many years later.

"While sleeping last night," he replied, "did I cease to abide in your home because I was unconscious of the fact? We should never be conscious of not abiding in Christ."

This was Hudson Taylor's spiritual secret—his life and ministry were changed dramatically by this profound truth in ways he could never imagine.

CHAPTER 15

NO MORE THIRST

What then? I am not careful to inquire:
I know there will be tears and fears and sorrow—
And then a loving Savior drawing nigher,
And saying, "I will answer for the morrow."
~ Selected

As months and years went by, the unsatisfied days never came back. Never again was his needy soul separated from the fullness of Christ. Trials came, deeper and more searching than ever before, but in them all joy flowed unhindered from the presence of the Lord himself. Hudson Taylor had found the secret of soul rest. Through this experience he had received a fuller understanding of the Lord Jesus as well as a fuller surrender and self-abandonment to him.

Hudson Taylor had been surrendered to Christ, but this was more; this was a new yieldedness, a glad, unreserved handing over of self and everything to him. It was no longer a question of giving up this or that if the Lord required it; it was a loyal and loving acceptance, a joyful meeting of his will in big and little things, as the very best that could be for his own. This made the trials of the following summer an opportunity for God's grace to triumph.

Even before the danger and excitement that culminated in the massacre of Tientsin in which 21 foreigners were killed, Hudson and

Maria Taylor had been called to pass through deep personal sorrow. It was time to make the most difficult decision they had ever had to make together—they decided that the time had come to part from their children and send them back to England. There were no schools in China where they could continue their education, and no places for refuge from the heat of summer. The climate and difficult living conditions they experienced took a toll on the children's health. They had already left their treasured Gracie buried in the soil of China, so they were thankful to accept the offer of their secretary and devoted friend, Miss Emily Blatchley, to take the three boys and only little girl to England and to care for them there.

The distance and separation was painful to anticipate. But even before the little travelers could be escorted to the coast, a longer parting still had to be faced. At only five years old, Samuel, the youngest of the boys, was the one whose health had suffered most. With concern, his parents saw that the strain of the coming separation was increasing his chronic trouble. All night they watched beside him on the boat that was taking them down the canal from Yangchow. But at dawn the following morning, he became unconscious, and there on the boat floating down the Yangtze River, he passed away.

In the midst of a driving storm, the Taylors crossed the river, which was about two miles wide at that point, to lay their young son in the cemetery at Chinkiang. From there they went on with the others to Shanghai. A few weeks later, after escorting them all on board the French mail ship which was to sail at daylight, Taylor wrote to Mr. Berger:

"I have seen them, awake, for the last time in China. About two of our little ones we have no anxiety. They rest in Jesus' bosom. And now, dear brother, though the tears will not be stayed, I do thank God for permitting one so unworthy to take any part in this great work, and do not regret having engaged in it. It is his work, not mine or yours; and yet it is ours—not because we are engaged in it, but because we are his, and one with him whose work it is."

This was the reality that sustained the Taylors. There had never been a more troubled summer in China than the summer of 1870. Yet in the midst of it all, with a longing for their children that was indescribable, they had never had more rest and joy in God.

"I could not but admire and wonder at the grace that so sustained and comforted the fondest of mothers," Taylor wrote as he recalled it afterwards. "The secret was that Jesus was satisfying the deep thirst of heart and soul."

Maria Taylor was at her best that summer. It seemed that she was carried on the tempest of troubles that raged around them. Many in the mission battled sickness, and before they could reach Chinkiang, after parting from the children, news reached them that Mrs. Judd was there and at the point of death. Taylor could not leave the boat because he was caring for another patient, but he consented to sending Maria on alone to give what help she could.

After days and nights of caring for his wife, Mr. Judd was almost at the end of his strength when he heard sounds in the courtyard below indicating an unexpected arrival. Who could it be at that time of night and where had they come from? No steamer had passed upriver, and native boats would not be traveling after dark.

There before him, having traveled all day in a wheelbarrow was Maria Taylor. He would not have hoped to see anyone else.

"Suffering though Mrs. Taylor was at the time," he recalled, "and worn with hard traveling, she insisted on my going to bed and that she would undertake the nursing. Nothing would induce her to rest.

"'No,' she said, 'you have quite enough to bear without sitting up at night any more. Go to bed, for I shall stay with your wife whether you do or not.'

"Never can I forget the firmness and love with which it was said— her face meanwhile shining with the tenderness of him in whom it was her joy and strength to abide."

God's affirmative response to persistent prayer brought the patient through, just as nothing but his attentiveness to their prayers saved the situation in many difficult situations that summer.

"We had previously known something of trial in one station or another," Hudson Taylor wrote to the friends of the mission, "but now in all simultaneously, or nearly so, a widespread excitement shook the very foundations of native society. It is impossible to describe the alarm and consternation of the Chinese when they first believed that native magicians were bewitching them, or their indignation and anger when told that these insidious foes were the agents of foreigners. It is well known how in Tientsin they rose and barbarously murdered the Sisters of Charity, the priests and even the French Consul. What then restrained them in the interior, where our brothers were alone, far from any protecting human power? Nothing but the mighty hand of God, in answer to united, constant prayer in the all-prevailing name of Jesus. And this same power kept us satisfied with Jesus—with his presence, his love, his providence."

It is easy to read of such experiences, but only those who have lived through similar times of danger can have any idea of the stress involved. The heat that summer was unusually severe and prolonged, which added to the unrest of the native population. Women and children had to be brought down to the coast, and for a time it seemed as though the Chinese authorities might require them to leave the country altogether. This involved a great amount of correspondence with officials, Chinese and foreign, and frequent letters to the workers in the most danger. The mission house at Chinkiang was completely full, and the situation was so stirred up that finding additional housing options was nearly impossible.

"Old times seem to be coming round again," Taylor wrote in June, referring to the Yangchow riot, "but with this difference, that our anxieties are not as before confined to one place."

By this time it looked as though they would have to give up all the river stations. The Taylors were living in Chinkiang because it was a more central location than Yangchow. He slept on the floor in the sitting-room or hallway so that she could share their room with other ladies.

"One difficulty follows another very fast," he continued after the Tientsin massacre,* "but God reigns, not chance. At Nanking the excitement has been frightful. ... Here the rumors are, I hope, passing away, but at Yangchow they are very bad. ... Pray much for us. My heart is calm, but my head is sorely tried by the constant succession of one difficulty after another."

But they chose not to allow the troubles of the time to hinder the spiritual side of the work. In the hottest days of June, Maria wrote to Miss Blatchley:

"We have been holding classes on Sunday and two or three evenings in the week, to interest the Chinese Christians who can read in searching the scriptures, and those who cannot read in learning to do so, and to set an example to the younger members of the mission who know pretty well that we have no lack of work. It may be a practical proof to them of the importance we attach to securing that the Christians and others about us learn to read and understand for themselves the word of God."

Hudson Taylor's newfound joy in his spiritual experience seems to have been deepened rather than hindered by the pressures of these days. His writings reveal not so much the difficulties and problems as the full tide of blessing that carried him through it all. After carefully answering her letter about Yangchow affairs, he wrote to Miss Desgraz, one of the workers:

"And now I have the very passage for you, and God has so blessed it to my own soul! John 7:37—'If any man thirst, let him come unto me and drink.' Who does not thirst? Who has not mind-thirsts, heart-thirsts, soul-thirsts or body-thirsts? Well, no matter which, or whether I have them all—'Come unto me and' remain thirsty? Ah no!

'Come unto me and drink.'

"What, can Jesus meet my need? Yes, and more than meet it. No matter how intricate my path, how difficult my service; no matter how sad my bereavement, how far away my loved ones; no matter how helpless I am, how deep are my soul-yearnings—Jesus can meet all, all, and more than meet. He not only promises me rest—ah, how welcome that would be, were it all, and what an all that one word embraces! He not only promises me drink to alleviate my thirst. No, better than that! 'He who trusts me in this matter (who believeth in me, takes me at my word), out of him shall flow ...' [John 7:38].

"Can it be? Can the dry and thirsty one not only be refreshed—the parched soil moistened, the arid places cooled—but the land be so saturated that springs well up and streams flow down from it? Even so! And not mere mountain-torrents, full while the rain lasts, then dry again ... but, 'from within him shall flow rivers'—rivers like the mighty Yangtze, ever deep, ever full. In times of drought brooks may fail, often do, canals may be pumped dry, often are, but the Yangtze never. Always a mighty stream, always flowing deep and irresistible!"

"Come unto me and drink" [John 7:37], he wrote in another June letter. "Not, come and take a hasty draught; not, come and slightly alleviate, or for a short time remove one's thirst. No! 'drink,' or 'be drinking' constantly, habitually. The cause of thirst may be irremediable. One coming, one drinking may refresh and comfort: but we are to be ever coming, ever drinking. No fear of emptying the fountain or exhausting the river!"

God had given him a source of comfort he would need to draw upon often that summer.

* * * * *

Six weeks later, joy and sorrow were strangely mingled in the missionary home at Chinkiang. A little son born to Hudson and Maria had filled their hearts with gladness. Almost immediately after the birth, however, Maria was hit with an attack of cholera and was unable to give nourishment to the infant. By the time a Chinese wet-nurse could be found, it was too late to save the little life. After only one week on earth he was taken home to heaven.

"Though excessively prostrated in body," Hudson Taylor wrote, "the deep peace of soul, the realization of the Lord's own presence and joy in his holy will with which she was filled, and which I was permitted to share, I can find no words to describe."

Maria chose the hymns to be sung at her own funeral, one of which, "O Holy Savior, Friend Unseen," had lingered in her mind.

Though faith and hope are often tried,
They ask not, need not aught beside;
So safe, so calm, so satisfied,
The souls that cling to Thee.
They fear not Satan or the grave,
They know Thee near and strong to save,
Nor fear to cross e'en Jordan's wave
While still they cling to Thee.

Even though she was very weak, it had not occurred to them that her days were numbered. The love that bound their hearts so closely prevented them from even thinking about being separated. Maria was only 33 and had always been quite strong. She had no pain in those final days of her life, only increasing weariness. Two days before the end, they received a letter from Mrs. Berger telling them that Miss Blatchley and the older children had arrived safely at Saint Hill. Maria savored every detail of their welcome and the arrangements for their well-being. She could not be thankful enough, and she seemed to have no desire but to praise God for his goodness. Mrs. Berger's letters had so often arrived at the moment when Maria needed them most, and so often the letters anticipated the circumstances in which they would be received, but never more so than with this letter.

"And now, farewell, precious friend," she wrote, "the Lord throw around you his everlasting arms."

It was in those arms she was resting.

"I never witnessed such a scene," wrote one who was present. "As dear Mrs. Taylor was breathing her last, Mr. Taylor knelt and committed her to the Lord, thanking him for having given her and for 12 and a half years of perfect happiness together, thanking him too for taking her to his own presence, and solemnly dedicating himself anew to his service."

The summer sun rose higher over the city, hills and river. The busy hum of life came up around them from the courts and streets. But in an upper room of one Chinese dwelling, from which the blue of heaven could be seen, there was the hush of a wonderful peace.

* * * * *

"Shall never thirst"—would it, could it prove true now? "To know that 'shall' means shall, that 'never' means never, and that 'thirst' means any unsatisfied need," Hudson Taylor often said in later years, "may be one of the greatest revelations God ever made to our souls." It was in these days of utter desolation that this promise was made so real in his breaking heart.

He wrote to his mother in August:

"From my inmost soul I delight in the knowledge that God does or permits all things, and causes all things to work together for good to those who love him.

"He and he only knew what my dear wife was to me. He knew how the light of my eyes and the joy of my heart were in her. On the last day of her life—we had no idea that it would be the last— our hearts were mutually delighted by the never-old story of each other's love ... and almost her last act was, with one arm round my neck, to place her hand on my head and, as I believe, for her lips had lost their cunning, to implore a blessing on me. But he saw that

132

it was good to take her—good indeed for her, and in his love he took her painlessly—and not less good for me who now must toil and suffer alone, yet not alone, for God is nearer to me than ever."

And to Mr. Berger he wrote: "When I think of my loss, my heart, nigh to breaking, rises in thankfulness to him who has spared her such sorrow and made her so unspeakably happy. My tears are more tears of joy than grief. But most of all I joy in God through our Lord Jesus Christ—in his works, his ways, his providence, himself. He is giving me to 'prove' (to know by trial) 'what is that good, and acceptable, and perfect, will of God' [Rom. 12:2]. I do rejoice in that will; it is acceptable to me; it is perfect; it is love in action. And soon, in that sweet will, we shall be reunited to part no more. 'Father, I will that they also, whom thou hast given me, be with me where I am' [John 17:24]."

Hudson Taylor walked in that faith, and yet when illness came with long, wakeful nights, he experienced grief.

"How lonesome," Taylor recalled "were the weary hours when confined to my room! How I missed my dear wife and the voices of the children far away in England! Then it was I understood why the Lord had made that passage so real to me, 'Whosoever drinketh of the water that I shall give him shall never thirst' [John 4:14]. Twenty times a day, perhaps, as I felt the heart-thirst coming back, I cried to him, 'Lord, you promised! You promised me that I should never thirst.'

"And whether I called by day or night, how quickly he came and satisfied my sorrowing heart! So much so that I often wondered whether it were possible that my loved one who had been taken could be enjoying more of his presence than I was in my lonely chamber. He did literally fulfill the prayer:

"Lord Jesus, make Thyself to me
A living, bright reality;
More present to faith's vision keen
Than any outward object seen;

More dear, more intimately nigh
Than e'en the sweetest earthly tie."

Among many letters of this period, few are more precious or revealing than those he managed to write to his children.

"You do not know how often father thinks of his darlings, and how often he looks at your photographs till the tears fill his eyes. Sometimes he almost fears lest he should feel discontented when he thinks how far away you are from him. But then the dear Lord Jesus who never leaves him says, 'Don't be afraid; I will keep your heart satisfied.' ... And I thank him, and am so glad that he will live in my heart and keep it right for me.

"I wish you, my precious children, knew what it is to give your hearts to Jesus to keep every day. I used to try to keep my own heart right, but it would always be going wrong. So at last I had to give up trying myself, and to accept the Lord's offer to keep it for me. Don't you think that is the best way? Perhaps sometimes you think, 'I will try not to be selfish or unkind or disobedient.' And yet, though you really try, you do not succeed. But Jesus says: 'You should trust that to me. I would keep that little heart, if you would trust me with it.' And he would, too.

"Once I used to try to think very much and very often about Jesus, but I often forgot him. Now I trust Jesus to keep my heart remembering him, and he does so. This is the best way. Ask dear Miss Blatchley to tell you more about this way, and pray God to make it plain to you, and to help you so to trust Jesus."

And to Miss Blatchley he wrote on the same subject, from the comfortless quarters of a coasting steamer:

"I have written again to the dear children. I do long for them to learn early ... the precious truths which have come so late to me concerning oneness with and the indwelling of Christ. These do not seem to me more difficult of apprehension than the truths about redemption. Both need the teaching of the Spirit, nothing more. May God help you to live Christ before these little ones, and to minister him to them. How wonderfully he has led and taught us! How little I believed the rest and peace of heart I now enjoy were possible down here! It is heaven begun below, is it not? ... Compared with this union with Christ, heaven or earth are unimportant accidents."

"Oh, it is joy to feel Jesus living in you," he wrote to his sister, Mrs. Walker, on the same journey, "to find your heart all taken up by him; to be reminded of his love by his seeking communion with you at all times, not by your painful attempts to abide in him. He is our life, our strength, our salvation. He is our 'wisdom, and righteousness, and sanctification, and redemption.' [1 Cor. 1:30] He is our power for service and fruit-bearing, and his bosom is our resting place now and forever."

Meanwhile, he still faced many outward difficulties. The political situation was more threatening than Taylor had ever known in China. The claims arising from the Tientsin massacre were still unsettled. The Chinese authorities, knowing that Europe was involved in war, ignored all of the issues that were brought before them. Taylor shared just how serious things had become in a letter in which he sent out a call for a day of fasting and prayer for all the mission's supporters on December 31. He wrote: "The present year has been in many ways remarkable. Perhaps every one of our number has been more or less face to face with danger, perplexity and distress. But out of it all, the Lord has delivered us. And some who have drunk more deeply than ever before of the cup of the Man of Sorrows can testify that it has been a most blessed year to our souls and can give God thanks for it. Personally, it has been the most sorrowful and the most blessed year of my life, and I doubt not that others have had in some measure the same experience. We have put to the proof the faithfulness of God—his power to support in trouble and to give patience under affliction, as well as to deliver from danger. And should greater dangers await us, should deeper sorrows come ... it is to be hoped that they will be met in a strengthened confidence in our God.

"We have great cause for thankfulness in one respect: we have been so situated as to show the Chinese Christians that our position, as well as theirs, has been and may again be one of danger. They have been helped, doubtless, to look from 'foreign power' to God himself for protection by the fact that (1) the former has been felt to be uncertain and unreliable ... and (2) that we have been kept in calmness and joy in our various positions of duty. If in any measure we have failed to improve for their good this opportunity, or have failed to rest, for ourselves, in God's power to sustain us in or protect us from danger, as he sees best, let us humbly confess this, and all conscious failure, to our faithful covenant-keeping God. ...

"I trust we are all fully satisfied that we are God's servants, sent by him to the various posts we occupy, and that we are doing his work in them. He set before us the open doors we have entered, and in past times of excitement he has preserved us. We did not come to China because missionary work here was either safe or easy, but because he had called us. We did not enter upon our present positions under a guarantee of human protection, but relying on the promise of his presence. The accidents of ease or difficulty, of apparent safety or danger, of man's approval or disapproval, in no wise affect our duty. Should circumstances arise involving us in what may seem special danger, we shall have grace, I trust, to manifest the depth and reality of our confidence in him, and by faithfulness to our charge to prove that we are followers of the Good Shepherd who did not flee from death itself. ... But is we would manifest such a spirit then, we must seek the needed grace now. It is too late to look for arms and begin to drill when in presence of the foe."

In regard to the ongoing financial needs of the mission, Taylor continued: "I need not remind you of the liberal help which the Lord has sent us direct, in our time of need, from certain donors, nor of the blessed fact that he abideth faithful and cannot deny himself.

If we are really trusting in him and seeking from him, we cannot be put to shame. If not, perhaps the sooner we find out the unsoundness of any other foundation, the better. The mission funds, or the donors, are a poor substitute for the living God."

Early in 1871, in addition to his grief, Hudson Taylor suffered a physical breakdown from liver and breathing problems that made him sleepless and led to painful depression. It was under these circumstances that he discovered fresh power and beauty in the promise of John 4:14: "but whoever drinks the water I give him will never thirst." The present tense of the Greek verb gave the suggestion of a continuous habit which flooded the passage with new meaning and met his long-continued need.

"Do not let us change the Savior's words," he often said in later years. "It is not 'Whosoever has drunk,' but 'Whosoever drinketh.' It is not of one isolated draught he speaks, or even many, but of the continuous habit of the soul. In John 6:35, also, the full meaning is, 'He who is habitually coming to me shall by no means hunger, and he who is believing on me shall by no means thirst.' The habit of coming in faith to him is incompatible with unmet hunger and thirst. ...

"It seems to me that where many of us err is in leaving our drinking in the past, while our thirst continues in the present. What we need is to be drinking—yes, thankful for each occasion which drives us to drink ever more deeply of the living water."

CHAPTER 16

OVERFLOW

In Thy strong hand I lay me down,
So shall the work be done;
For who can work so wondrously
As the Almighty One?
~ Selected

In the testing days of 1870, Hudson Taylor was still a young man in his thirties, and the China Inland Mission numbered only 33 members. They had opened mission stations in three provinces and converts gathered into 10 or 12 little churches. It was still a day of small things; yet the burden was heavy when it was carried by only one man—and he was already weary from so many challenging years in China.

By the end of 1871, it became clear that Mr. and Mrs. Berger, who had so generously cared for the home side of the mission, could no longer continue with their work. Their health was failing and they were spending their winters abroad. They intended to sell Saint Hill, the beautiful home they had used as the headquarters for the China Inland Mission, and all the correspondence, account keeping and editorial work, the testing of candidates and practical management of business details needed to be passed on to others. Even though the Bergers were still supportive and passionate about the work, it was with a sense of almost desolation that Taylor took over their responsibilities. It was clear he must remain in England for a time.

Taylor moved the headquarters from Saint Hill to Pyrland Road, a little suburban street in the north of London. The quarters were small and not very impressive. Downsizing from Mr. Berger's library to the small back room which had to do duty both as study and office was not an easy task. During this time of change and what must have seemed like a set back, Hudson Taylor wrote: "My path is far from easy. I never was more happy in Jesus, and I am very sure he will not fail us; but never from the foundation of the mission have we been more cast upon God. It is well, doubtless, that it should be so. Difficulties afford a platform upon which he can show himself. Without them we could never know how tender, faithful and almighty our God is. ... The change about Mr. and Mrs. Berger has tried me not a little. I love them so dearly! And it seems another link severed with the past in which my precious departed one, who is seldom absent from my thoughts, had a part. But his word is, 'Behold, I make all things new' [Rev. 21:5]."

It must have been difficult for Taylor to settle into the routine of office work as he longed to press forward with the great task before them in China. Since he had no indication about what the Lord had in view, he was not in a rush to make new plans. But when prayer for the right helpers seemed to bring no answer, and the work to be done kept him from what he was tempted to regard as more important matters, it would have been easy to be impatient or discouraged. Even with things in that state, he wrote to a fellow missionary in China:

"It is no small comfort to me to know that God has called me to my work, putting me where I am and as I am. I have not sought the position and I dare not leave it. He knows why he places me here— whether to do, or learn, or suffer. 'He that believeth shall not make haste' [Is. 28:16]. That is no easy lesson for you or me; but I honestly think that 10 years would be well spent, and we should have our full value for them, if we thoroughly learned it in them. ... Moses seems to have been taken aside for 40 years to learn it. ... Meanwhile, let us beware alike of the haste of the impatient, impetuous flesh, and of its disappointment and weariness."

God used this time in Taylor's life to bring about very fruitful ministry. As he faithfully carried out his office work, he also had opportunity to meet many new people and share about his work. In the busy world of London, a bright young man, Frederick Baller, had given his heart to the Lord and wanted to learn about opportunities for life work in China. He made his way to Pyrland Road where he found himself in the plainly furnished room where people were gathering for the prayer meeting.

"A large text," he recalled, "faced the door by which we entered, 'My God shall supply all your need' [Phil. 4:19], and as I was not accustomed to seeing texts hung on walls in that way, it decidedly impressed me. Between a dozen and 20 people were present. ...

"Mr. Taylor opened the meeting by giving out a hymn, and seating himself at the harmonium, led the singing. His appearance did not impress me. He was slightly built, and spoke in a quiet voice. Like most young men, I suppose I associated power with noise, and looked for physical presence in a leader. But when he said, 'Let us pray,' and proceeded to lead the meeting in prayer, my ideas underwent a change. I had never heard anyone pray like that. There was a simplicity, a tenderness, a boldness, a power that hushed and subdued me, and made it clear that God had admitted him to the inner circle of his friendship. Such praying was evidently the outcome of long tarrying in the secret place, and was as dew from the Lord.

"I have heard many men pray in public since then, but the prayers of Mr. Taylor and the prayers of Mr. [Charles] Spurgeon stand all by themselves. Who that heard could ever forget them? It was the experience of a lifetime to hear Mr. Spurgeon pray, taking as it were the great congregation of 6,000 people by the hand and leading them into the holy place. And to hear Hudson Taylor plead for China was to know something of what is meant by 'the effectual fervent prayer of a righteous man' [James 5:16]. That meeting lasted from four to six o'clock, but seemed one of the shortest prayer meetings I had ever attended."

From the west of England, an educated young woman named Miss H. E. Soltau had come to London to attend the Mildmay Conference, and she was staying as a guest at Pyrland Road. She was among the 2-3,000 people crowded into the hall who heard Taylor give the opening address. Impressed as she was when she saw how he influenced Christian leaders, it was the everyday life of his work at the mission house that really struck her. He bore the burdens and met the tests of faith with daily joy in the Lord.

"I remember Mr. Taylor's exhortation," she wrote much later, "to keep silent to all around and let our wants be known to God only. One day, when we had had a small breakfast and there was scarcely anything for dinner, I was thrilled to hear him singing the children's hymn: 'Jesus loves me, this I know, for the Bible tells me so.' Then he called us together to praise the Lord for his changeless love, to tell our needs and claim the promises. And before the day was over we were rejoicing in his gracious answers."

Far from being discouraged by the funding shortfalls after Mr. Berger's retirement, Taylor was looking forward, determined to press on with the goals of the China Inland Mission. Standing before the big map of China one day at Pyrland Road, he turned to a few friends who were with him and said, "Have you faith to join me in laying hold upon God for 18 men to go two and two to the nine unevangelized provinces?" That little group joined hands before the map, determined to pray daily for the 18 evangelists needed. There was no doubt about the faith. But how little any of them dreamed of the wider expansion that was coming, of the important part Miss Soltau would play in the development of the mission, or of the unique service to be rendered by Frederick Baller—both drawn to the work at this time through the unconscious overflow of Hudson Taylor's life.

So the waiting time was fruitful, and when Taylor was able to return to China, he left behind him an experienced council of friends in London in addition to Miss Blatchley in charge of his home and children at Pyrland Road. They only had 21 pounds in hand, but there was no debt, and it was with confidence that Taylor wrote to the friends of the China Inland Mission:

"Now that the work has grown, more helpers are needed at home, as abroad, but the principles of action remain the same. We shall seek pecuniary aid from God by prayer, as heretofore. He will put it into the hearts of those he sees fit to use to act as his channels. When there is money in hand, it will be remitted to China; when there is none, none will be sent; and we shall not draw upon home, so that there can be no going into debt. Should our faith be tried as it has been before, the Lord will prove himself faithful as he has ever done. Nay, should our faith fail, his faithfulness will not—for it is written, 'If we believe not, yet he abideth faithful' [2 Tim. 2:13]."

Never was this confidence more needed than when, after an absence of 15 months, Hudson Taylor once again landed in China. The work was discouraging in several of the older centers that had encountered sickness and other challenges. The little churches were not what they had been, stations were understaffed, some even closed, and Taylor hardly knew where to begin to give the help and encouragement that was badly needed. Instead of planning for advance to unreached provinces, it was all he could do to build up the existing work.

Thankfully God had given him a devoted companion. Miss Jenny Faulding, the much-loved leader of the women's work in Hangchow, had become his second wife. They were often parted, though, because Taylor went on the most physically difficult journeys without her.

"I have invited the church members and inquirers to dine with me tomorrow," he wrote from one closed station. "I want them all to meet together. May the Lord give us his blessing. Though things are sadly discouraging, they are not hopeless; they will soon look up, by God's blessing, if they are looked after."

Those words "things will soon look up, by God's blessing, if they are looked after" were very characteristic of the practical nature of Taylor's faith. He went on prayerfully and patiently to the most difficult places, depending on the power of the Spirit, to straighten out difficulties and infuse new passion into the new believers and missionaries. He and Jenny also spent three months together in Nanking directing evangelism.

"Every night we gather large numbers by means of pictures and lantern slides," he wrote from that city, "and preach to them Jesus. ... We had fully 500 in the chapel last night. Some did not stay long; others were there nearly three hours. May the Lord bless our stay here to souls. ... Every afternoon women come to see and hear."

In and through it all, God was sustaining them in their ministry. He wrote this question in a letter to Miss Blatchley: "If you are ever drinking at the fountain, with what will your life be running over?—Jesus, Jesus, Jesus!"

This overflow was just what Taylor needed as he visited every mission station at least once as well as nearly every outstation of the China Inland Mission. As he went, he also sought out the Chinese leaders in each place. He personally assisted the evangelists, teachers and women who taught the Bible in whatever way he could. When they could be together, Jenny's assistance was invaluable. They would often work together far into the night catching up with correspondence. She was often his companion on medical journeys, sometimes remaining at one station where there was sickness while he went on to another.

Since there was no other doctor in the mission or anywhere

away from the treaty ports, Taylor's medical knowledge was a blessing wherever he went. Needless to say, this also created a lot of additional work when he reached a distant station to find 98 letters of all kinds waiting for him. He usually took time the very next day to respond, but whether it meant longer letters or extra journeys, he was thankful for any and every way in which he could help. To be "the slave of all" (Mark 10:44) was the privilege he desired most.

"The Lord is prospering us," he was able to write after about nine months, "and the work is steadily growing, especially in that most important department, native help. The helpers themselves need much help, much care and instruction; but they are becoming more efficient as well as more numerous, and the hope for China lies doubtless in them. I look on foreign missionaries as the scaffolding round a rising building; the sooner it can be dispensed with the better— or the sooner, rather, that it can be transferred to serve the same temporary purpose elsewhere."

In the stress of needs at hand, especially when funds for the existing work were never enough, it would have been easy to lose the sense of urgency about the great needs that were still unmet. But with Hudson Taylor, just the reverse was the case. Traveling from place to place on the long journeys between the stations through populous country teeming with friendly, accessible people, his heart went out more and more to the unreached, both near and far.

"Last week I was at Taiping," he wrote to the council in London. "My heart was greatly moved by the crowds that literally filled the streets for two or three miles, so that we could hardly walk, for it was market day. We did but little preaching, for we were looking for a place for permanent work, but I was constrained to retire to the city wall and cry to God to have mercy on the people, to open their hearts and give us an entrance among them.

"Without any seeking on our part, we were brought into touch with at least four anxious souls. An old man found us out, I know not how, and followed me to our boat. I asked him in and inquired his name.

"'My name is Dzing,' he replied. 'But the question which distresses me, and to which I can find no answer, is—what am I to do with my sins? Our scholars tell us that there is no future state, but I find it hard to believe them. ... Oh, sir, I lie on my bed and think. I sit alone in the daytime and think. I think and think and think again, but I cannot tell what is to be done about my sins. I am 72 years of age. I cannot expect to finish another decade. 'Today knows not tomorrow's lot,' as the saying is. Can you tell me what to do with my sins?'

"'I can indeed,' was my reply. 'It is to answer this very question that we have come so many thousands of miles. Listen, and I will explain to you what you want and need to know.'

"When my companions returned, he heard again the wonderful story of the cross, and left us soothed and comforted ... glad to know that we had rented a house and hoped soon to have Christian colporteurs [literature distributers] resident in the city."

In that one province of Zhejiang there were more than 50 cities without any witness for Christ that needed the same work. And beyond that were millions more! Alone there in his boat, Hudson Taylor could only cast the burden on the Lord. His faith was strengthened, and in one of his Bibles he made this entry on January 27, 1874:

"Asked God for 50 or 100 additional native evangelists and as many missionaries as may be needed to open up the four Fus and 48 Hsien cities still unoccupied in Zhejiang, also for men to break into the nine unoccupied provinces. Asked in the name of Jesus.

"I thank thee, Lord Jesus, for the promise whereon thou hast given me to rest. Give me all needed strength of body, wisdom of mind, grace of soul to do this thy so great work."

What followed, however, was not added strength, but a serious illness. Week after week he lay in helpless suffering, only able to hold on in faith to the heavenly vision. Funds had been so low for months that he had scarcely known how to distribute the little that came in, and there was nothing at all in hand for beginning anything new. But, "we are going on to the interior," he had written to the secretaries in London. "I do so hope to see some of the destitute provinces evangelized before long. I long for it by day and pray for it by night. Can he care less?"

Advance had never seemed more impossible. But in the Bible before him was the record of that transaction of his soul with God, and in his heart was the conviction that, even for inland China, God's time had almost come. And then as he lay there slowly recovering, he received a letter from an unknown correspondent which had been sent two months earlier from England.

"My dear Sir," the somewhat trembling hand had written, "I bless God—in two months I hope to place at the disposal of your council, for further extension of the China Inland Mission work, 800 pounds. Please remember, for fresh provinces. ...

"I think your receipt form beautiful: 'The Lord our Banner'; 'The Lord will provide.' If faith is put forth and praise sent up, I am sure that Jehovah of Hosts will honor it."

Eight hundred pounds for "fresh provinces"! Taylor could hardly believe it. The very secrets of his heart seemed to look back at him from that sheet of foreign notepaper. Even before the prayer was recorded in his Bible, that letter had been sent off; and now, just when most needed, it had reached him with its wonderful confirmation. Then God's time had surely come!

The letter so encouraged him that he was soon recovered enough to get from his sickroom back to the Yangtze valley. Many gathered that spring in Chinkiang. There, as in almost all the stations, new life had come to the Chinese Christians. New believers were joining the churches, and native leaders were growing in zeal and usefulness. Older missionaries were encouraged, even with great need all around them, and young men who had made good progress with the language were eager for pioneering work. Taylor called together a conference, and whoever could leave their stations came together for a week of prayer and meetings before he and Mr. Judd set out up the Yangtze to find a base from which they could begin a western branch of the mission.

"Is it not good of the Lord so to encourage us," Taylor wrote from Chinkiang, "when we are sorely tried from want of funds?"

It was not an abundance of supplies that had brought them new joy and hope. He wrote to a close Christian friend:

"Never has our work entailed such real trial or so much exercise of faith. The sickness of our beloved friend, Miss Blatchley, and her strong desire to see me; the needs of our dear children; the state of funds; the changes required in the work to admit of some going home, others coming out, and of further expansion, and many other things not easily expressed in writing, would be crushing burdens if we were to bear them. But the Lord bears us and them too, and makes our hearts so very glad in himself—not himself plus a bank balance—that I have never known greater freedom from care and anxiety.

"The other week, when I reached Shanghai, we were in great and immediate need. The mails were both in, but no remittance! And the folios showed no balance at home. I cast the burden on the Lord. Next morning on waking I felt inclined to trouble, but the Lord gave me a word—'I know their sorrows, and am come down to deliver' [Ex. 3:7-8]; 'Certainly I will be with thee' (v. 12)—and before 6 a.m. I was as sure that help was at hand as when, near noon, I received a letter from Mr. Müller which had been to Ningpo and was thus delayed in reaching me, and which contained more than 300 pounds.

"My need now is great and urgent, but God is greater and more near. And because he is and is what he is, all must be, all is, all will be well. Oh, my dear brother, the joy of knowing the living God, of seeing the living God, of resting on the living God in our very special and peculiar circumstances! I am but his agent. He will look after his own honor, provide for his own servants, and supply all our need according to his own riches, you helping by your prayers and work of faith and labor of love."

A note to Jenny Taylor of about the same time (April, 1874) breathed the same confidence: "The balance in hand yesterday was 87 cents. The Lord reigns; herein is our joy and rest!" And to Mr. Baller he added, when the balance was still lower, "We have this—and all the promises of God."

"Twenty-five cents," recalled the latter, "plus all the promises of God! Why, one felt as rich as Croesus, and sang:

I would not change my blest estate
For all the earth holds good or great;
And while my faith can keep its hold,
I envy not the sinner's gold."

The hymn of the conference that spring in Chinkiang was, "In some way or other the Lord will provide," and it was with this in mind that Taylor wrote to Miss Blatchley:

"I am sure that, if we but wait, the Lord will provide. ... We go shortly, that is, Mr. Judd and myself, to see if we can procure headquarters at Wuchang, from which to open up western China as the Lord may enable us. We are urged on to make this effort now, though so weak handed, both by the need of the unreached provinces and by our having funds in hand for the work in them, while we have none for general purposes. ... I cannot conceive how we shall be helped through next month, though I fully expect we shall be. The Lord cannot and will not fail us."

And yet, at that very time, they faced new difficulties and delays. Brave and faithful to the last, Miss Blatchley's health had given way under her many responsibilities. The Taylor children at Pyrland Road needed care, and the home side work of the mission was almost at a standstill. After Mr. Judd was established at Wuchang, Hudson and Jenny Taylor hurried home to England. But even before they could leave China, the beloved friend they hoped to see one last time passed away.

The homecoming a few weeks later was strange and sorrowful. Finding Miss Blatchley's place empty, the children scattered and the weekly prayer meeting discontinued was disheartening. But even so, they had not reached the lowest point. On his way up the Yangtze with Mr. Judd, Hudson Taylor had taken a fall which caused serious injury. Concussion of the spine develops slowly, and it was not until he had been at home some weeks that the rush of London life began to show the extent of the problem. He began to experience gradual paralysis of the lower limbs that completely confined him to his bed. Laid aside in the prime of life, he could only lie in that upstairs room, conscious of all there was to be done, of all that was not being attended to—lie there and rejoice in God.

Yes, rejoice in God! With desires and hopes as limitless as the needs that pressed upon his heart, with the prayer he had prayed and the answers God had given, with opportunities opening in China and a wave of spiritual blessing reviving the churches at home that he longed to see turned into missionary channels, and with little hope, humanly speaking, that he would ever stand or walk again, the deepest thing was joy in the will of God as "good, pleasing and perfect" (Rom. 12:2). It is certain that from that place of suffering sprang all the larger growth of the China Inland Mission.

A narrow bed with four posts was the sphere to which Hudson Taylor was now restricted. But, there, between the posts at the foot of the bed was the map! The map of the whole of China hung at his feet and round about him, day and night, was the presence of God to which he had access in the name of Jesus. Long after, when prayer had been fully answered and the pioneers of the China Inland

Mission were preaching Christ far and wide throughout those inland provinces, a leader of the Church of Scotland said to Taylor, "You must sometimes be tempted to be proud because of the wonderful way God has used you. I doubt if any man living has had greater honor."

"On the contrary," was the earnest reply, "I often think that God must have been looking for someone small enough and weak enough for him to use, and that he found me."

* * * * *

The outlook did not brighten as the year drew to a close. Hudson Taylor was less and less able to move and could only turn in bed with the help of a rope fixed above him. At first he had managed to write a little, but now he could not even hold a pen. Then, at the beginning of 1875, a little paper found its way into the Christian press entitled: "Appeal for Prayer: On Behalf of More than a Hundred and Fifty Millions of Chinese." It briefly stated the facts about the nine unevangelized provinces and the aims of the China Inland Mission. It reported that 4,000 pounds had recently been given for the special purpose of sending the gospel to these distant regions. Chinese Christians were ready to take part in the work. The urgent need was for more missionaries who were willing to face any hardship in leading the way.

"Will each of you Christian readers," it continued, "at once raise his heart to God, spending one minute in earnest prayer that God will raise up, this year, 18 suitable men to devote themselves to this work?"

The appeal did not say that the leader of the China Inland Mission was by all appearances a hopeless invalid. It did not refer to the fact that the 4,000 pounds had come from his wife and himself, part of their capital, the whole of which they had consecrated to the work of God. It did not mention the covenant of two or three years previously to pray in faith for the 18 evangelists until they should be given. But those who read the paper felt there was much behind it, and they were moved in ways that only come when things are rooted deeply in God.

In no time at all the Taylors received far more correspondence, and with the increase came an increase of his joy in dealing with it—or in seeing how the Lord dealt with it.

"The mission had no paid helpers," he wrote of this time, "but God led volunteers, without prearrangement, to come in from day to day, to write from dictation. If one who called in the morning could not stay long enough to answer all letters, another was sure to come, and perhaps one or two might look in, in the afternoon. Occasionally a young friend employed in the city would come in after business hours and do needful bookkeeping, or finish letters not already dealt with. So it was day by day. One of the happiest periods of my life was that period of forced inactivity, when one could do nothing but rejoice in the Lord and 'wait patiently' [Ps. 37:7] for him, and see him meeting all one's need. Never were my letters, before or since, kept so regularly and promptly answered.

"And the 18 asked of God began to come. There was first some correspondence, then they came to see me in my room. Soon I had a class studying Chinese at my bedside. In due time the Lord sent them all forth; and then dear friends at Mildmay began to pray for my restoration. The Lord blessed the means used, and I was raised up. One reason for my being laid aside was gone. Had I been well and able to move about, some might have thought that my urgent appeals, rather than God's working, had sent the 18 men to China. But utterly laid aside, able only to dictate a request for prayer, the answer to our prayers was the more apparent."

God also provided in amazing ways as answers to prayers about funds at this time. The monthly remittance to be cabled to China on one occasion was very small, nearly 235 pounds less than what was usually needed to cover the expenses. The specific need was brought before the Lord in prayer, and in his goodness the answer came quickly. That very evening the postman brought a letter which contained a check to be entered, "From the sale of plate"—and the sum was just over 235 pounds.

When Taylor was finally able to be up and about again, he was returning from a meeting when he was boldly approached by a Russian nobleman who had heard him speak. As they traveled to London together, Count Bobrinsky took out his pocketbook.

"Allow me to give you a trifle," he said, "toward your work in China."

The banknote handed to Hudson Taylor was for a large sum, and the latter realized that there must be some mistake.

"Did you not mean to give me five pounds?" he questioned; "please let me return this note, it is for 50!"

"I cannot take it back," replied the count, no less surprised. "Five pounds was what I meant to give, but God must have intended you to have 50. I cannot take it back."

Impressed with what had taken place, Taylor reached Pyrland Road to find the household gathered for special prayer. A China remittance was to be sent out, and the money in hand was short by 49 pounds. Taylor laid his banknote for 50 pounds on the table. Could it have come more directly from God's hand?

But even with all the answers to prayer during these years, the way was far from open to inland China. There came a time after the 18 pioneers had been sent out when it seemed that nothing could prevent war over the murder of a British official. Negotiations had dragged on for months, but the Chinese government would not give in to any of the demands. The British ambassador, exhausting all his diplomatic possibilities, left Beijing. The atmosphere was tense and seemed on the brink of war as friends of the China Inland Mission tried to discourage Taylor from sailing with a party of eight new workers.

"You will all have to return," they said. "And as to sending off pioneers to the more distant provinces, it is simply out of the question."

Was there some mistake? Had the men and the money been given in vain? Was inland China still to remain closed to the gospel?

In the third-class cabin of that French steamer there was a man on his knees, dealing with God. "My soul yearns, oh how intensely," he had written two years previously, "for the evangelization of the 180 million of these unoccupied provinces. Oh, that I had 100 lives to give or spend for their good!" All that lay in his power he had done, keeping the vision undimmed through every kind of discouragement. What would happen now?

But God's time had indeed come. At the last moment, a change came over the Chinese Foreign Office. The viceroy, Li Hung-chang, hurried to the coast, catching up to the British minister at Chefoo. Finally the memorable "Chefoo Convention"* was signed (in 1876) which gave free access, at last, to every part of China.

"Just as our brethren were ready," Taylor delighted to recall, "not too soon and not too late, the long-closed door opened to them of its own accord."

CHAPTER 17

WIDER OVERFLOW

Oh, Christ, he is the fountain,
The deep, sweet well of love;
The streams on earth I've tasted,
More deep I'll drink above.
~ A. R. Cousin

Within the next two years the China Inland Mission pioneers traveled 30,000 miles throughout the inland provinces of China sharing the good news of Christ's redeeming love. This brought Taylor one of the biggest tests of faith he ever had to meet. The country proved wonderfully open, and it was natural, after years of hardship in preparing the way, that the young missionaries should wish to establish homes of their own from which to work as settled centers. This, of course, meant homemakers. Several of the pioneers were engaged to be married and were waiting for Taylor's approval to take the first white women as their fellow workers to the far interior. They could not foresee, perhaps, as their leader could, all that would be involved, and that before long, other women would have to take those difficult journeys to continue work begun by busy mothers in those distant homes.

Years before, however, Taylor had faced it all and had set out on the policy of encouraging women's work. The outcry was tremendous, as he knew it would be, when he sanctioned the first departure of married couples to the far interior. Missionary work in China was taking on a new phase that called for new sacrifices and new demands on faith and endurance.

But the situation developed gradually. For a year or more the criticism Taylor had to face was directed against the widespread travels of the pioneers. These journeys by foot or wheelbarrow were difficult. There were dangers and disappointments to record as well as glorious encouragement. "Conflicts on the outside, fears within" (2 Cor. 7:5), and Taylor, detained at Chinkiang by the administrative work of the mission, was glad to be there to guide or give strength when needed.

The secret of his strength was quite evident. Whenever work permitted, Taylor refreshed himself by playing a little harmonium and singing hymns. His favorite contained the words: "Jesus, I am resting, resting, in the joy of what Thou art; I am finding out the greatness of Thy loving heart."

One of the 18 evangelists, George Nicoll, was with him on one occasion when some letters were handed in to his office, bringing news of serious rioting in two of the older mission stations. Thinking that Taylor might wish to be alone, the younger man was about to withdraw when, to his surprise, someone began to whistle. It was the soft refrain of the same well-loved hymn: "Jesus, I am resting, resting, in the joy of what thou art ..."

Turning back, Mr. Nicoll could not help exclaiming, "How can you whistle, when our friends are in so much danger?"

"Would you have me anxious and troubled?" was the quiet reply. "That would not help them, and would certainly incapacitate me for my work. I have just to roll the burden on the Lord."

Day and night this was his secret, "just to roll the burden on the Lord." Those who were awake in the little house in Chinkiang at two or three in the morning would frequently hear the soft refrain of Taylor's favorite hymn. He had learned that, for him, only one life was possible—just that blessed life of resting and rejoicing in the Lord under all circumstances, while he dealt with the difficulties, inward and outward, great and small.

* * * * *

After 16 months in China, Hudson Taylor returned once again to London. He returned knowing that 6 million people in North China were facing starvation, and they lived in a province in which there were no missionaries except a few China Inland Mission pioneers. Children were dying by the thousands and young girls were being sold into slavery and carried away in troops to cities farther south. Taylor had come home burdened to do all in his power to mobilize urgent relief work. God had provided the funds for the rescue of children, but where was the woman who could go to that stricken province to undertake the work? No white woman had ever been beyond the mountains that separated Shanxi Province from the coast, and to get there required a two-week journey by mule litter over dangerous roads and with miserable inns at night.

Taylor had been home with his wife and family only a few months when this urgent need caused them to separate once again. Jenny was sensing that God would have her reach these lost and dying ones. A little worn notebook recalls the experiences through which her faith was strengthened as she waited upon God to know whether or not the call was really from him. But once she did know, not even the sacrifice involved for her husband, whose suggestion it had been, held her back. Jenny went and left behind her family of seven—two little ones of her own, four older children and an adopted daughter. Who would care for them? She brought all her hard questions to God, and he not only answered them, meeting every need as it arose, but gave grace for the parting and all the difficult, dangerous work in China.

"Cross-loving men are needed," Taylor had written before coming home. "Oh, may God make you and me of this spirit. ... I feel so ashamed that you and the dear children should affect me more than millions here who are perishing—while we are sure of eternity together."

After that, it was easier for Taylor to let other women join the front ranks because his own wife had led the way. Part of his reward when they were reunited a year later (1879) was to have her with him in China as, in province after province of the interior, women's work quietly opened up.

The story of those years is fascinating and heart moving. Wrecked in the Yangtze gorges, the first women who went to the far west spent a strange Christmas amid their bridal belongings spread out to dry upon the rocks. Everywhere they went the crowds overwhelmed them.

"For nearly two months past," Mrs. Nicoll wrote from Chungking, "I have seen some hundreds of women daily. Our house has been like a fair."

More than once she fainted from weariness in the midst of her guests—the only white woman in a province of some 60 million people—returning to consciousness to find the women fanning her, full of affection and concern. One lady, who cared for her like a mother, would send out her own sedan chair with an urgent request for Mrs. Nicoll to return in it immediately. The most comfortable bed in her own apartment was waiting, and, after sending out all the younger women, she would sit down herself to fan the weary visitor until she fell asleep. After she rested, she was given an inviting dinner—on no account was Mrs. Nicoll allowed to leave until she had eaten a proper meal.

That was the surprise that awaited the first women everywhere they went—the people were glad to see them and eager to hear their message, showing not only natural curiosity but real heart sympathy. God blessed them in amazing ways! By the end of the second year after missionary women came on the scene, the pioneers were rejoicing in 60 or 70 converts gathered into little churches in the far inland provinces.

Emily King became the first one to make the three-month journey up the Han River to go to the women of the Northwest. She also was the first to give her life in the effort, dying of typhoid fever in the city of Hanchung (May 1881). But before her brief course ended, she had the joy of seeing no fewer than 18 women baptized in confession of their faith in Christ. That is why she went and what lifted her above the grief of leaving her husband desolate and their little one motherless.

Having lost his own Maria to the demands and disease of the work, no one understood better than Hudson Taylor the cost at which such work was done. In that understanding, he devoted himself to it with unfailing prayer.

"I cannot tell you how glad my heart is," he wrote to his mother in the midst of much trial, "to see the work extending and consolidating in the remote parts of China. It is worth living for and worth dying for."

After that, developments were rapid and wonderful. But associated with every fresh advance, every access of power and blessing, there was in Hudson Taylor's own experience a corresponding period of suffering and trial. With each one he was plunged deeper and deeper into life with God alone. Outwardly it may have seemed, at times, that the work was carried on a flood tide of success. Glorious steps of faith were taken; glorious answers to prayer were received. But only those who shared them behind the scenes understood the preparation of heart beforehand and the steady burden bearing afterwards.

One stands silenced before such profound heart searchings, such trials of faith and such exercise of soul. Being prepared to go all lengths with God, prepared to die daily in quiet, practical reality, prepared to be the servant of his brothers (least of all and servant of all), prepared to stand for them in ceaseless intercession, not only bearing with their failures and weaknesses, but bearing them up in creative faith and love that lifted to higher levels—this is the only way spiritual success can be possible.

Before the forward movement which had brought new life to the work—when women missionaries first went inland—there had been a period of intense and prolonged suffering. Three times in 1879 Taylor's life was in danger through serious sicknesses, and in the year that followed, while the new line of things was being tested and established by God's blessing, the China Inland Mission was faced with intense and accumulated trials. Jenny Taylor touched upon a deep principle when she wrote at that time:

"Don't you think that if we set ourselves not to allow any pressure to rob us of communion with the Lord, we may live lives of hourly triumph, the echo of which will come back to us from every part of the mission? I have been feeling these last months that of all our work the most important is that unseen, upon the mount of intercession. Our faith must gain the victory for the fellow workers God has given us. They fight the seen and we must fight the unseen battle. And dare we claim less than constant victory, when it is for him, and we come in his name?"

But times of trial, as by a spiritual law, always led on to increase and blessing. That was the case when, after parting from Jenny who could no longer be spared from home, Taylor headed west to meet with some of the younger workers. He wrote to her:

"You are ploughing the Mediterranean and will soon see Naples. ... I am waiting for a steamer to Wuchang. I need not, cannot tell you how much I miss you, but God is making me feel how rich we are in his presence and love. ... He is helping me to rejoice in our adverse circumstances, in our poverty, in the retirements from our mission. All these difficulties are only platforms for the manifestation of his grace, power and love.

"I am very busy," he continued from Wuchang when the meetings had begun. "God is giving us a happy time of fellowship together, and is confirming us in the principles on which we are acting."

That one brief sentence, taken in connection with the crisis to which they had come, lets in a flood of light upon the important sequel to those days of fellowship at Wuchang. For unconsciously to the younger missionaries, it was a crisis, and more was hanging in the balance than Taylor himself could realize. After years of prayer and patient, persevering effort, a position of unparalleled opportunity had been reached. Inland China lay open before them. At all the settled stations in the far north, south and west, reinforcements were needed. Not to advance would be to retreat from the position of faith taken up at the beginning. It would be to look at difficulties rather than at the living God. True, funds were low, had been for years, and the new workers coming out were few. It would have been easy to say, "For the present, no further extension is possible." But not to go forward would be to cripple and hinder the work; to throw away opportunities God had given, and before long to close stations opened at great cost. This, surely, could not be his way for the evangelization of inland China.

What then was the outcome of those days of quiet waiting upon God? It was a step of faith so startling that, for a time, the sympathy of friends at home seemed doubtful. For it was no less than an appeal to the home churches—later on signed by almost all the members of the China Inland Mission—for 70 new workers to be sent out within the next three years. The entire membership of the mission numbered barely 100 and they had been low on funds for such a long time. Yet, the group at Wuchang was so sure of being guided of God in their definite prayer and expectation that one of them exclaimed, "If only we could meet again and have a united praise meeting, when the last of 'The Seventy' have reached China!"

They agreed that three years was the period in which they should look for the answer (1882-84) as it would hardly be possible to receive and arrange for so many new workers in a shorter time.

"We shall be widely scattered then," said another, of a practical turn of mind. "But why not have the praise meeting now? Why not give thanks for 'The Seventy' before we separate?"

This was approved and they held the meeting so that all who had joined in the prayer also united in the thanksgiving.

And "The Seventy" were given, wonderfully given, in the next three years. But faith was thrown into the crucible in many ways. The trials they faced regarding funds continued, but the trials about the work itself were even more challenging. And yet Taylor was able to write:

"I do feel more and more the blessedness of real trust in God. Faith, he tries, but sustains. And when our faithfulness fails, his remains unshaken. 'He cannot deny himself' [2 Tim. 2:13]. ...

"The Lord Jesus, this year of very peculiar trial from almost every quarter, does make my heart well up and overflow with his love. He knows what separations and other incidents of our service mean, and he so wonderfully makes all loss to be gain! ... Excuse my running on in this way. My glad heart seems as if it must have vent, even among figures and remittances."

As the first of the three years in which they were seeking "The Seventy" wore on, it became evident that there were serious misgivings at home in England about the appeal. Taylor was at Chefoo at the time, and he felt in his heart that he was to ask the Lord to put his seal on the matter in a way that could not be mistaken. It was at one of the daily prayer meetings, on or about the second of February, and the few who were present felt quite free to lay this request before God.

One who was present wrote: "We knew that our Father loves to please his children, and we asked him lovingly to please us, as well as to encourage timid ones at home, by leading some one of his wealthy stewards to make room for a large blessing for himself and his family by giving liberally to this special object."

A few days later Hudson Taylor sailed for England, and it was not until he stopped at Aden that he learned the result. No account of that special prayer meeting had been sent home; but at Pyrland

Road they had had the joy of receiving on the second of February a sum of 3,000 pounds, with the words: "Ask of me, and I shall give thee the heathen for thine inheritance, and the uttermost parts of the earth for thy possession" (Psalm 2:8). This was punctuated by the fact that the gift was sent in an unusual way—the names of five children were added to those of the parents. What could have been more encouraging than to see how literally God answered prayer?

It was the same some years later, when they took another great step forward in faith.

God had so blessed with the going out of "The Seventy" that the mission had been lifted on to a new plane of influence at home. During those years the pioneering character of the work had become known. "They are opening up the country," wrote Alexander Wylie of the London Missionary Society, "and this is what we want. Other missions are doing a good work, but they are not doing this work." Christian hearts were deeply stirred when John McCarthy reached England after walking across China, from east to west, preaching Christ all the way; when John Stevenson and Dr. Henry Soltau came home, the first to enter western China from Burma (Myanmar), following the Yangtze River to Shanghai; and then when they were joined in England by Hudson Taylor with the appeal for 70 new workers.

The way had been prepared by the devoted labors of Taylor's brother-in-law, Benjamin Broomhall, who for seven years had represented the China Inland Mission in London, and who, with Amelia Broomhall, made its headquarters at Pyrland Road a center of love and prayer. With a genius for friendship and a heart to embrace the whole church of God, Broomhall found openings in many directions for the testimony of the mission. People were anxious to hear how the seemingly impossible had been brought to pass, and how without appeals for money, or even collections, the growing work was sustained.

"If you are not dead yet," was the charming communication of a child at Cambridge to whom "Hudson Taylor" was a household word,

"I want to send you the money I have saved up to help the little boys and girls of China to love Jesus."

"Will you do me the kindness," urged Canon Wilberforce of Southampton, "to give a Bible-reading in my house to about 60 people ... and spend the night with us? Please do us this favor, in the Master's name."

"Much love to you in the Lord," wrote Lord Radstock from the Continent. "You are a great help to us in England by strengthening our faith."

From Dr. Andrew Bonar came 100 pounds forwarded from an unknown Presbyterian friend "who cares for the land of Sinim." Charles Spurgeon invited him to speak at the Tabernacle, and Miss Macpherson invited him to Bethnal Green.

"My heart is still in the glorious work," wrote Mr. Berger with a check for 500 pounds. "Most heartily do I join you in praying for 70 more laborers—but do not stop at 70! Surely we shall see greater things than these, if we are empty of self, seeking only God's glory and the salvation of souls."

And Mr. Berger's faith was justified: "Surely we shall see greater things than these." "The Seventy" as God gave them, proved to be an overflowing answer to prayer. Before the last party sailed, they had been overtaken by the well-known "Cambridge Band," whose consecrated testimony before they left England swept the British universities with a profound spiritual movement which reached on and out to the ends of the earth. It was a rising tide of spiritual blessing, and the new edition of China's Spiritual Need and Claims, which Taylor had somehow found the time to publish, deepened and continued the work.

Before the Cambridge party could sail, detained as they were by revival in university centers, Taylor went on ahead to China, missing the final farewell meeting at Exeter Hall. The contrast could hardly have been more marked between the enthusiasm of that great gathering for all the China Inland Mission stood for and the solitary man alone upon his knees, day after day, in the cabin of the ship that was carrying him back to the stern realities of the fight. "Borne on a great wave of fervent enthusiasm," as the editorial secretary of the Church Missionary Society expressed it, the work had been swept into a new place in the sympathy and confidence of the Lord's people. "The mission has become popular," Mr. Broomhall was writing, not without concern. But out in China, Hudson Taylor had to face the other side of that experience.

"Soon we shall be in the midst of the battle," he wrote from the China Sea, "but the Lord our God in the midst of us is mighty—so we will trust and not be afraid. 'He will save' [Zeph. 3:17]. He will save all the time and in everything."

And again, some months later he wrote to his wife: "Flesh and heart often fail: let them fail! He faileth not. Pray very much, pray constantly, for Satan rages against us. ....

"There is much to distress. Your absence is a great and ever-present trial, and there is all the ordinary and extraordinary conflict. But the encouragements are also wonderful—no other word approaches the truth, and half of them cannot be told in writing. No one dreams of the mighty work going on in connection with our mission. Other missions too, doubtless, are being greatly used. I look for a wonderful year."

With its outstanding answers to prayer leading up to the next forward movement, 1886 was a wonderful year.

Taylor had spent several months visiting inland districts where many of the new workers were located. He had traveled through Shanxi holding conferences which were reported in a little book entitled Days of Blessing. The quiet power of his life and testimony opened up to younger workers the deep things of God and encouraged those he met. When Taylor met Pastor Hsi, the converted Confucian scholar, for the first time, they conferred together about the future of the work with mutual love and appreciation.

"We all saw visions at that time," recalled John Stevenson who was with them. "Those were days of heaven upon earth. Nothing seemed difficult."

Coming down the Han River on the last stage of this journey, it was quite natural for Taylor to take charge of Annie, a five-year-old girl whose missionary parents realized that only a change to the coast could save the child's life. There was no woman in the party, and they knew that for a month or six weeks little Annie would have no one to care for her, day or night, except Hudson Taylor. But they were more than satisfied.

"My little charge is wonderfully improving," he was able to write from the boat. "She clings to me very lovingly, and it is sweet to feel little arms about one's neck once more."

Straight from this journey, Taylor came to the first meeting of the China Council of the mission. The newly appointed superintendents of the provinces gathered at Anking, including John Stevenson and John McCarthy. They gave a whole week to prayer and fasting, so that they would face the important issues before them with prepared hearts. Hudson Taylor came with fresh reports and the desire to lead toward growth and development, but even he was startled by the suggestion that grew out of the conference—that for anything like the increase and advance they were describing to occur, they urgently needed 100 new workers.

After examining every detail of the plans laid out, Taylor had at last to agree that with 50 central stations and China open before them from end to end, 100 new workers in the following year would not be enough. John Stevenson, by this time deputy director of the mission, was full of faith and courage. He sent a communication explaining the situation to all the members of the mission and cabled to London with Taylor's permission—"Praying for 100 new workers in 1887."

But what a thrill that meant at home! A hundred new recruits for China in one year? No mission in existence had ever dreamed of sending out reinforcements on such a scale. The China Inland Mission then numbered only 190 members; and to pray for more than a 50 percent increase within the next 12 months—well, people almost held their breath! But only until Hudson Taylor came home. "Strong in faith, giving glory to God," he brought a spiritual uplift that was soon felt throughout the fellowship of the mission. The three-fold prayer they were praying in China was taken up by countless hearts: that God would give the 100 workers, those of his own choice; that he would supply the 50,000 dollars of extra income needed, no appeal or collections being made; and that the money might come in in large sums to keep down correspondence, a practical point with a small office staff.

And what happened in 1887? Six hundred men and women actually offered to join the mission in that year, of whom 102 were chosen, equipped and sent out. Not 50, but $55,000 extra was actually received, without solicitation, so that every need was met. And how many letters had to be written and receipts made out to acknowledge this large sum? Just 11 gifts covered it all, which added very little to the work of the staff members who were already giving all they could to meet other needs. And best of all, wherever the story of "The Hundred" became known, it strengthened faith and stirred hearts with new and deeper longings.

One unexpected result was a visit to London by Henry W. Frost, a young American businessman who was also an evangelist, upon whose heart it had been laid to invite Hudson Taylor to come to the United States. Frost was so sure that his visit to England for this purpose had been guided of God that the disappointment when Taylor did not respond was overwhelming. Drawn to the China Inland Mission by all he had seen and heard, and to Hudson Taylor in particular, he returned to New York perplexed, feeling that his mission had been in vain. But God's working in the matter had only just begun.

The following summer (1888) Taylor did visit America and was received by D. L. Moody and the leaders of the Niagara Bible

Conference, among others. Surprising developments took place in answer to prayer—chiefly the prayers of Henry Frost that went up from the heart that had known such disappointment and was now rejoicing to see the hand of God working far beyond anything he had asked or thought.

When Hudson Taylor went on to China, three months later, he did not go alone. Fourteen young men and women accompanied him, a precious gift of God to the China Inland Mission. Various denominations were represented, both from the United States and Canada, and the gifts and prayers so unexpectedly called forth were just the beginning of a steady stream which has flowed out for China ever since. The interest was so great that they had to form a North American Council. At a large sacrifice to himself and his family, Henry Frost, whom God had used to bring it all to pass, undertook to represent and guide the work. It was one of the most fruitful developments to which the Lord ever led in connection with Taylor's ministry, and he went on to meet all that was to grow out of it filled with new faith and courage.

This represented a great step forward—from that time onward the China Inland Mission, which had always been interdenominational, became international. Hudson Taylor remained in active service for 12 more years, and they were years of worldwide ministry. A visit to Scandinavia opened to him the warm hearts of Swedish and Norwegian Christians; Germany sent devoted teams to work in association with the mission; Australia and New Zealand welcomed Taylor as one long known and loved, and the China Council in Shanghai became the center of a greater organization than its founder had ever imagined.

The spiritual overflow of those last years was best of all—just the same streams of blessing, only reaching now to the ends of the earth. The impressions of an Episcopalian minister who was Taylor's host in Melbourne:

"He was an object lesson in quietness. He drew from the bank of heaven every farthing of his daily income—'My peace I give unto you' [John 14:27]. Whatever did not agitate the Savior or ruffle his spirit was not to agitate him. The serenity of the Lord Jesus concerning any matter, and at its most critical moment, was his ideal and practical possession. He knew nothing of rush or hurry, or quivering nerves or vexation of spirit. He knew that there is a peace passing all understanding, and that he could not do without it. ...

"'I am in the study, you are in the big spare room,' I said to Mr. Taylor at length. 'You are occupied with millions, I with tens. Your letters are pressingly important, mine of comparatively little moment. Yet I am worried and distressed, while you are always calm. Do tell me what makes the difference.'

"'My dear Macartney,' he replied, 'the peace you speak of is, in my case, more than a delightful privilege, it is a necessity. I could not possibly get through the work I have to do without the peace of God 'which passeth all understanding' [Phil. 4:7] keeping my heart and mind.'

"That was my chief experience of Mr. Taylor. Are you in a hurry, flurried, distressed? Look up! See the man in the glory! Let the face of Jesus shine upon you—the wonderful face of the Lord Jesus Christ. Is he worried or distressed? There is no care on his brow, no least shade of anxiety. Yet the affairs are his as much as yours.

"'Keswick teaching,' as it is called, was not new to me. I had received those glorious truths and was preaching them to others. But here was the real thing, an embodiment of 'Keswick teaching'* such as I had never hoped to see. It impressed me profoundly. Here was a man almost 60 years of age, bearing tremendous burdens, yet absolutely calm and untroubled. Oh, the pile of letters! Any one of which might contain news of death, of lack of funds, of riots or serious trouble. Yet all were opened, read and answered with the same tranquility—Christ his reason for peace, his power for calm. Dwelling in Christ, he drew upon his very being and resources, in the midst of and concerning the matters in question. And this he did by an attitude of faith as simple as it was continuous.

"Yet he was delightfully free and natural. I can find no words to describe it save the scriptural expression 'in God.' He was in God all the time and God in him. It was that true 'abiding' of John 15. But oh, the lover-like attitude that underlay it! He had in relation to Christ a most bountiful experience of the Song of Solomon. It was a wonderful combination—the strength and tenderness of one who, amid stern preoccupation, like that of a judge on the bench, carried in his heart the light and love of home.

"And through it all, the vision and spiritual urgency of earlier years remained unchanged. Indeed the sense of responsibility to obey the last command of the Lord Jesus Christ only increased, as he came to see more clearly the meaning of the Great Commission."

"I confess with shame," Taylor wrote as late as 1889, "that the question, what did our Lord really mean by his command to 'preach the gospel to every creature' [Mark 16:15] had never been raised by me. I had labored for many years to carry the gospel further afield, as have many others; had laid plans for reaching every unevangelized province and many smaller districts in China, without realizing the plain meaning of our Savior's words.

"'To every creature'? And the total number of Protestant communicants in China was but 40,000. Double that number, treble it, to include adherents, and suppose each one to be a messenger of light to eight of his own people—and, even so, only one million would be reached."

"To every creature"—the words burned into his very soul. But how far was the church, how far had he been himself from taking them literally, as intended to be acted upon?

"How are we going to treat the Lord Jesus Christ," he wrote under deep conviction, "with regard to this last command? Shall we definitely drop the title 'Lord' as applied to him? Shall we take the ground that we are quite willing to recognize him as our Savior, as far as the penalty of sin is concerned, but are not prepared to own ourselves 'bought with a price' [1 Cor. 6:20], or Christ as having claim to our unquestioning obedience? ...

"How few of the Lord's people have practically recognized the truth that Christ is either Lord of all or he is not Lord at all! If we can judge God's word, instead of being judged by it, if we can give God as much or as little as we like, then we are lords and he is the indebted one, to be grateful for our dole and obliged by our compliance with his wishes. If, on the other hand, he is Lord, let us treat him as such. 'Why call ye me, Lord, Lord, and do not the things which I say?' [Luke 6:46]."

So, all unexpectedly, Hudson Taylor came to the widest outlook of his life, the purpose which was to dominate the closing years of its active leadership: nothing less than a definite, systematic effort to do just what the Master commanded; to carry the glad tidings of his redeeming love to every man, woman and child throughout the whole of China. He did not think that the China Inland Mission could do it all. But he did believe that with proper division of the field the missionary forces of the church were well equal to the task.

* * * * *

But he did not see it in his day. With the willing cooperation of the mission, movement began in Kiangsi and plans were maturing for advance all over the field. But in the providence of God, a deep baptism of suffering had to come first. The Boxer Rebellion* of 1900 broke out, and madness swept the country, with the China Inland Mission more exposed to its fury than any other. Taylor had just reached England after a serious breakdown in health, and under a feeling of concern that she hardly understood, Jenny Taylor persuaded him to go on to a quiet spot in Switzerland where his health had been restored some years previously.

It was in this quiet setting that the upsetting news came to him. Telegram after telegram came telling of riots, massacres, and the hunting down of refugees in station after station of the mission. The news kept coming and it bore down on him physically and emotionally until he thought he could take no more. Had he not gone to the protection of the remote valley where news could be given to him in measured amounts, Hudson Taylor would have been himself among those whose lives were laid down for Christ's sake and for China in the sweeping horror of that summer. As it was, he lived through it, holding on to God.

"I cannot read," he said when things were at their worst; "I cannot pray, I can scarcely even think—but I can trust."

* * * * *

The Boxer crisis passed, but not before thousands had died, including 58 China Inland Mission members, 21 of their children and many of those who had become believers through the work of the mission. Even in this context as the members returned to their work, the calm words of a white-haired pastor in Shansi came true: "Kingdoms may perish," he said, almost with his last breath, "but the church of Christ can never be destroyed."

In this confidence, he and thousands of other Chinese Christians sealed their testimony with their blood; and in this confidence, the witness of faithful lives that had been spared began again.

D. E. (Dixon Edward) Hoste, whom Hudson Taylor had appointed as his successor, dealt so wisely with the situation that enemies were turned to friends and the Chinese authorities quickly expressed their appreciation of a literal carrying out of the commands of Christ which meant more, from their point of view, than all the preaching that had gone before.

Hudson Taylor lived to see the new day of opportunity opening in China and to return to the land of his love and prayers. But he returned alone. Jenny Taylor, his beloved companion of many years, died of cancer in 1904. She had been such a blessing and had so brightened the closing days of their pilgrimage together. Though heavy with grief, early in the next year he turned his face once more toward China. At 73 years old he traveled with his son and daughter-in-law on one of the most remarkable journeys of his lifetime.

As he traveled throughout the country, passing from station to station, missionaries and Chinese Christians gathered to love and revere him. They welcomed him as "China's Benefactor," the one through whom the gospel had reached those inland provinces. After traveling up the Yangtze River to Hankow and spending some weeks in the northern province of Hunan, Taylor was strengthened to take one more journey. He had never expected to find himself in Hunan. As the first of the nine unevangelized provinces where pioneers of the China Inland Mission had gone, it had proved by far the most difficult. Taylor had prayed for that province for more than 30 years, and it was fitting that the last rich joy to come to him should be to welcome Hunan converts.

The Christians gathered eagerly in the capital, at the home of Dr. Frank Keller and were looking forward to Sunday services with the beloved leader of whom they had heard so much. The Kellers had lovingly hosted a reception for him with the missionaries in the city on Saturday, June 3, 1905. But it was that evening the call came. Hudson Taylor passed away quietly in his room. It was hardly death—just the glad, swift entry upon life eternal.

And the very room seemed filled with unutterable peace.

CHAPTER 18

STREAMS FLOWING STILL

He told me of a river bright
That flows from him to me,
That I might be, for his delight,
A fair and fruitful tree.
~ Gerhard Tersteegen

When Hudson Taylor was caught away from the heart of China—passing in one painless moment to the presence of the Lord he loved—a feeling almost of suspense held many hearts. "What will become of the China Inland Mission now?" was the unspoken question. Hudson Taylor was a man of such unusual faith. What would happen without his presence and leadership? The thought was natural, but years have only proved that though the father and long-loved leader of the work passed on, the God in whom he was confident remains.

The lines of the hymn by Tersteegen were dear to Taylor and express the essence of his spiritual secret.

"It is very simple," he wrote, "but has he not planted us by the river of living water that we may be, for his delight, fair and fruitful to his people?"

God was first in Hudson Taylor's life—not the work, not the needs of China or of the China Inland Mission and not his own experiences. He knew that the promise was true, "Delight yourself in the Lord; and he will give you the desires of your heart" (Psalm 37:4). This promise is just as true today. Miss Soltau's words can reflect the hearts of many: "The work is always increasing, and were it not for the consciousness of Christ as my life, hour by hour, I could not go on. But he is teaching me glorious lessons of his sufficiency, and each day I am carried forward with no feeling of strain or fear of collapse."

Streams flowing still—how true it has been in the experience of the enlarged and ever-growing mission! The main facts as to the developments of the last 30 years are given in an appendix, and wonderful facts they are. But here we would only refer—as we turn from the past to the present—to the practical side of Hudson Taylor's spiritual life. He knew that the thought expressed by Oswald Chambers is true: "God does not give us overcoming life: He gives us life as we overcome." To him, the secret of overcoming lay in daily, hourly fellowship with God; and this, he found, could only be maintained by secret prayer and feeding upon the word.

It was not easy for Hudson Taylor to make time for prayer and Bible study, but he knew that it was vital. His children recall traveling with him month after month in northern China, by cart and wheelbarrow, with the poorest of inns at night. Often with only one large room for coolies and travelers alike, they would screen off a corner for their father and another for themselves, with curtains of some sort; and then, after sleep at last had brought a measure of quiet, they would hear a match struck and see the flicker of candlelight which told that Taylor, however weary, was poring over the little Bible that he always had with him. He usually prayed from two to four in the morning because this was the time when he could be most sure of being undisturbed as he waited upon God. That flicker of candlelight has meant more to them than all they have read or heard on secret prayer; it meant reality, not preaching but practice.

The hardest part of a missionary career, Hudson Taylor found, is to maintain regular, prayerful Bible study. "Satan will always find you something to do," he would say, "when you ought to be occupied about that, if it is only arranging a window blind."

He would have fully endorsed Andrew Murray's weighty words: "Take time. Give God time to reveal himself to you. Give yourself time to be silent and quiet before him, waiting to receive, through the Spirit, the assurance of his presence with you, his power working in you. Take time to read his word as in his presence, that from it you may know what he asks of you and what he promises you. Let the word create around you, create within you a holy atmosphere, a holy heavenly light, in which your soul will be refreshed and strengthened for the work of daily life."

It was just because he did this that Hudson Taylor's life was full of joy and power, by the grace of God. One day when he was over 70 years old, he paused as he crossed the sitting room in Lausanne, Bible in hand, and said to one of his children: "I have just finished reading the Bible through, today, for the fortieth time in 40 years." And he not only read it, he lived it.

Hudson Taylor stopped at no sacrifice in following Christ. "Cross-loving men are needed," he wrote in the midst of his labors in China, and if he could speak to us today would it not be to call us to that highest of all ambitions: "that I may know him, and the power of his resurrection and the fellowship of his sufferings" (Phil. 3:10). Can we not hear again the tones of his quiet voice as he says:

"There is a needs-be for us to give ourselves for the life of the world. An easy, non-self-denying life will never be one of power. Fruit-bearing involves cross-bearing. There are not two Christs—an easy-going one for easy-going Christians, and a suffering, toiling one for exceptional believers. There is only one Christ. Are you willing to abide in him, and thus to bear much fruit?"

APPENDIX A

(1932, DR. HOWARD AND GERALDINE TAYLOR)

When Hudson Taylor laid down the leadership of the China Inland Mission (CIM) in 1900, five years before he died, the CIM numbered 750 missionaries. In 1932, when this book was first published, its membership was 1,285. The income while Hudson Taylor was directing the work and sustaining it with his prayers ran to more than 4 million dollars—requested from God alone. The total income between 1900 and 1932 was almost 20 million dollars—requested from God alone. And there was no debt. In rich answer to Hudson Taylor's prayers, 700 Chinese workers were connected with the mission, and 13,000 converts had been baptized. In 1932 there were nearly 4,000 Chinese workers connected with the CIM and in the years between 1900 and 1932 there were 100,000 baptisms. "Not us, O Lord, not us, but to your name be the glory" (Ps. 115:1).

As the founder as well as director of the CIM, Hudson Taylor was unique in his relation to the work. No one, in this sense, could take his place. Yet, in the leader God raised up to follow him, the gift was just as unique. While under the guidance of D. E. Hoste, through years of storm and stress, the work went steadily on from strength to strength.

True, there were times of overwhelming trial and apparent setback. When the revolution broke out and China, almost overnight, became a republic, a reign of terror prevailed in certain districts and the CIM was again called to add to its martyr roll. In the city of Sian, once capital of the empire, Mrs. Beckman and six children of missionary families, as well as Mr. Vatne who was trying to protect them, were murdered by a lawless mob. Scores of missionaries were forced to leave their stations for places of greater safety; others, who held on, were enabled to protect many of the terrified people around them, women especially, who fled to the missionary homes for refuge. In those days there were many precious opportunities to live as well as preach the gospel, and the friendly feeling toward missionaries in the interior was very marked.

With the spread of lawlessness and cruel banditry, as well as the organized agitation among students, missionaries and Chinese Christians alike faced great and increasing dangers. But the amazing thing was that changes so stupendous could take place without more bloodshed and upheaval. Swept away from all the old moorings, reaching out with passionate desire for better things, China in her helplessness fell among thieves. The desperate counsels of communism and Bolshevism prevailed in many places, and the relentless aggressions of neighboring powers added to the distresses of the situation.

"When brothers fall out," the old Chinese proverb has it, "then strangers are apt to take advantage of them"; again, "to complete a thing, 100 years is not sufficient; to destroy, one day is more than enough."

Yet in the midst of it all, the protecting hand of God was over the work, so that advance was steady in connection with the evangelistic program of the CIM. The fact that the work is evangelistic rather than institutional accounts for much of the friendliness of the people and their readiness to listen to the gospel. In the early 1930s opportunities to sell Christian literature and give witness to the saving power of Christ were unprecedented. "The healing of his seamless dress" ("Serenity," a hymn by John Greenleaf Whittier) is the healing that China needs, and many are the wounded hearts turning to him for life and hope amid conditions of despair.

That such an hour is no time for retrenchment in the missionary enterprise must be manifest to all who look to God, who "look up," rather than at circumstances. This is what called the China Inland Mission of the 1930s out from a policy of waiting into a glorious advance along the lines of Hudson Taylor's latest and greatest vision. With regard to the fresh realization that came to him of the Lord's plain meaning in his definite commission, "Preach the gospel to every creature" (Mark 16:15, kjv), Taylor had written: "This work will not be done without crucifixion, without consecration which is prepared at any cost to carry out the Master's command. But given that, I believe in my inmost soul that it will be done.

"If ever in my life I was conscious of being led of God, it was in the writing and publication of those papers [To Every Creature]."

Living seed, though it falls to the ground and dies, will yet bring forth fruit. Hudson Taylor had long gone to his reward when a second baptism of suffering was permitted in the overwhelming distress of 1927. More than 600 members of the mission were forced to evacuate their stations in that tragic year, when western governments, alarmed at a new and fierce outbreak of anti-foreign agitation, ordered their nationals to withdraw from the interior.

"This was inspired by propagandists from Moscow," as Dr. Robert H. Glover, then the North American Director of the China Inland Mission, writes, "who incited the Chinese soldiery and student body to acts of violence, particularly directed against missionaries and other foreigners. ... And so the large majority of missionaries all over China were forced to leave their stations, their beloved converts and the work of years, and make their way to the coast. Thus, almost before they were aware of it, several hundred CIM missionaries, among others, found themselves out of inland China, with the door closed behind them."

To provide for these refugees in the overcrowded settlements imposed a heavy burden on the funds of the mission. They had to rent and furnish 14 houses in Shanghai alone, and all the traveling expenses had to be met out of strained resources. Many supporters of the mission at home, seeing that the work was for the time being largely at a standstill, found other channels for their missionary giving. Had the China Inland Mission been depending on its donors rather than on the living God, the outcome might have been very far from what it was. But "God is equal to all emergencies," as Hudson Taylor loved to remind himself and others, and his dealings with the CIM in the financial crisis of 1927 constitute one of the most marvelous answers to prayer that the CIM has ever known.

The following are the facts. The income of the CIM fell off in that one year not by thousands but by tens of thousands of dollars. With largely increased demands upon its resources, and with strict adherence to its principles of making no appeal for financial help and of never going into debt, how was the situation to be met—with an income diminished by no less than $114,000?

"God is equal to all emergencies"; and that year he was pleased to work in an unexpected way. Money transmitted to China from the home countries has to be changed into silver currency at a rate which is always fluctuating. But that year the fluctuation, strange to say, seemed steadily in favor of the mission funds. More and more silver was available for purchase with the money remitted from home, and by the close of the year it was found that while $114,000 less had been sent to China than in the previous year, the CIM had profited on exchange as much as $115,000! God met all the needs, and that year of special trial became one of overflowing praise.

And as to the matter of the closed door, Dr. Glover continues:

"It was indeed a sad hour ... and the outlook from the human point of view was dark enough. Would the door of missionary opportunity ever reopen? The question was variously answered ... [by the skeptical, the worldly-wise, and the discouraged]. But there were missionaries—and those of the CIM happily among the number—whose anointed eye saw the situation in a very different light.

"That the blow came directly from Satan, and with intent to ruin the work of missions, they doubted not. But did the word anywhere teach that God's servants were ever to accept defeat at the hands of Satan? Assuredly not. Had Satan at any time succeeded through persecution in destroying the cause of Christ? Far from it. ... Paul, the great missionary, testified that the persecutions which befell him had 'fallen out rather unto the progress of the gospel' [Phil. 1:12], and he followed on to exhort his fellow workers to be 'in nothing terrified by your adversaries' [Phil. 1:28]. Nothing in the New Testament missionary record is more impressive than the way opposition and persecution from the enemy were repeatedly made by God the very means of advancing the missionary enterprise. Every such assault of the adversary today, therefore, should become the occasion of a forward movement issuing in fresh expansion and enlarged results."

That is just the way the China Inland Mission was led to regard the adverse situation with which it was confronted. Was missionary work in China at an end? How could it possibly be, with Christ's Great Commission unrevoked, and the task of giving the gospel to China's millions still so very far from completed? At whatever cost, the work must go on. And so the mission went upon its face before God in fervent prayer for the reopening of the door and for clear guidance as to its future plans.

"Those were days of deep heart searching," Dr. Glover goes on to testify, "as well as of earnest prayer. And it was then, right in the midst of the trial, that God gave vision and conviction for a great advance. For it was then that, on the basis of a comprehensive survey of the whole CIM field, the leaders of the mission felt clearly led to appeal to God and his people for, not 100, but 200 additional workers for a forward movement of a strongly evangelistic character."

The constituency of the mission at home was impressed and rejoiced when they received this appeal. It was recognized to be of God, the outcome of much prayer, and at once new life was felt in all parts of the work. The two years in which the new missionaries were expected, not only asked for, passed quickly (1929-31), and though faith was tried in various ways, not least by strong counterattacks of the adversary in China, the story has been one of profound encouragement and blessing.

Not only did 1931 witness the outgoing of the last parties of the "Two Hundred"—91 of whom were from North America—but the provision made for their reception in China was no less remarkable. The headquarters of the mission in Shanghai, which had long been inadequate for the needs of the work, were replaced during that year by a much larger, more suitable situation which God provided without the cost of a single cent to the mission. An opportunity came, in answer to much prayer, to sell the old premises, the gift of a member of the mission now with the Lord, for 65 times their original cost. And the new buildings were ready in time to receive the more than 100 new workers who arrived in China for the China Inland Mission in the brief period of one month in the fall of 1931.

Much more was included in that wonderful provision than the wisest leaders in the CIM could foresee. In early 1932 the Japanese forces made their unexpected attack on Shanghai. Much of the fighting centered in and around the very district (Hongkew) in which the former headquarters of the China Inland Mission had been located. The guiding hand of God led to the change which moved the mission premises three miles farther back into the international settlement, to a position of greater safety, just in time. Who but he could have foreseen and provided in this wonderful way to meet this distressing situation?

God is still caring for the needs of his own work. Little wonder that the China Inland Mission stands firmly on the old truths upon which it was founded; little wonder that it commemorates with thankfulness the centenary this year, 1932, of the birth of its father in God, the leader whose faith and obedience brought it into being. Thank God, there is not one of its 1,285 missionaries who cannot and does not joyfully reiterate the conviction of its founder: "The living God still lives, and the living word is a living word, and we may depend upon it. We may hang upon any word God ever spoke or caused by his Holy Spirit to be written."

Oh, make but trial of his love;
Experience will decide
How blest are they, and they alone,
Who in his truth confide.
Fear him, ye saints, and you will then
Have nothing else to fear;
Make but his service your delight,
Your wants shall be his care.

"The past has not exhausted the possibilities nor the demands for doing great things for God. The church that is dependent on its past history for its miracles of power and grace is a fallen church. ... The greatest benefactor this age could have is the man who will bring the teachers and the church back to prayer."

E. M. Bounds, Power Through Prayer.

APPENDIX B

2010, GWEN HANNA

At its peak in 1939, the China Inland Mission (CIM) had more than 1,300 missionaries, and nearly 200,000 Chinese and minority people had been baptized. During the years of World War II and those that followed, missionaries had fantastic opportunities among university students and professionals, some of whom were high up in the government. The benefit to the church of these years of war is difficult to assess. It was a time of great harvest, and a preparation for the difficult days when the communist armies with their atheistic emphasis would be in control.

Many missions pulled out in 1948-49, but the CIM was one which attempted to stay. Having so decided, the CIM took a further step of faith and brought in 49 new workers to Shanghai in 1948 and in 1949. But it eventually became plain that the continued presence of the missionaries was causing suspicion and harassment for the Chinese believers. So the momentous decision was made in 1950 that in the best interests of the Chinese church, the CIM would withdraw.

The CIM now faced the question of whether it should continue to exist. Was this to be the end, or was there something new in God's plan? It was either extinction or expansion. Discovering great pockets of need that included totally unreached people groups in the countries surrounding China, the CIM decided God wanted them to move forward in new faith. The mission began again in East Asia, establishing headquarters in Singapore.

A new name, Overseas Missionary Fellowship (OMF), was adopted in 1964 (changed again to OMF International in 1993) and the old name (China Inland Mission) was dropped. Asian Christians also began to be accepted into membership during this period, and home councils were formed in Japan, Korea, Singapore, Hong Kong, Malaysia, the Philippines, Taiwan and Indonesia. Today, nearly 20% of OMF International's membership comes from Asia.

In 2006 Dr. Patrick Fung became the general director, the first Asian believer to hold this position for OMF International. At the OMF International Council gathering in 2006 he presented "Passion for the Impossible—Reaching the Neglected Frontiers," to leaders from across the countries and fields where OMF serves. In his keynote, Dr. Fung looked at lessons from the China Inland Mission (CIM) history, its recent past and ministry priorities for the next 5-10 years.

He stressed the importance of who OMF International is as a fellowship: a godly community, a pioneering mission, a relevant organization and a caring family with a servant spirit. He then presented an outline of key concepts for OMF International as they look to the future.

Considering the totality of the effort required, OMF International's leaders forged "The Five Challenges." These identified the kind of workers God can use; the work they would do; the number of new workers needed to join the effort; how to process them and, finally, how to partner with the churches involved.

OMF International's international leadership invested a tremendous amount of energy into discerning God's call to the neglected frontiers. They performed a detailed survey, a contemporary version of the one done with Hudson Taylor in 1883, of all the fields in East Asia. Leaders in China, Japan, Laos, Macau and so on reported on people groups and workers and all that God was doing. The momentum built as each shared the physical and spiritual needs of the targeted peoples and the numbers of personnel needed in the work. God led to the "impossible" tally of a need for 900 new workers for the work at hand! These workers will teach, provide medical expertise, lead in business ventures and a wide variety of other means to bring the gospel.

At the close of the gathering, OMF International's leaders left with a passion for these impossible challenges:

1. To pursue holiness.
2. To reach the neglected frontiers.
3. To pray for 900 new workers by 2110 (including 200 support workers).
4. To assess, care for and equip our people.
5. To engage with the sending church in fresh ways.

The nations of East Asia are still teeming with thousands who need to receive those "glad tidings" that Hudson Taylor sought to bring to the furthest points of China, and God is still leading OMF International. In 2010 (at the printing of this book), OMF International has nearly 3,000 from 36 nations working from home side offices and throughout East Asia. OMF International is still breaking new ground in the most dramatically changing region of the world—whether in outreach to more than 100 people groups, working with disadvantaged children, seeking new ways of evangelizing the unreached of Manila, teaching and influencing students in Taiwan and Indonesia, pioneering a witness among the Malays in South Thailand, translating the Bible, or living as 'salt and light' (Matthew 5:13-14) in countries closed to traditional missionary service. OMF International's missionaries are giving their energies towards building a strong church in the countries of East Asia.

In our fast-paced global world, it is a challenge to know how to become purposefully involved in God's global plan. Things have changed so rapidly. Months-long trips by boat to faraway destinations have been replaced with 24-hour airline hops between cultures done by students, business people and leisure travelers. Photos and artifacts carried home in trunks have been replaced with live video and daily blogs. Week-long mission events have often been replaced by "mission moments." We live in a time when discovering purposeful involvement in God's affairs around the world requires us to be so much more intentional. Instead of letting the amazing work of God in the world pass by like yesterday's headlines or a click of the TV remote, we need to engage intentionally.

By reading this inspiring story of a life well lived, you have seen at least in part what it takes to reach a nation with God's good news. Some, like Hudson Taylor with his family or the Cambridge Seven or "the Seventy," are called to go and learn the language and adapt to the culture and use whatever means God provides to share his truth. Some, like the Broomhalls, are called to send ... minding the business at home to keep those on the field equipped and encouraged. God's economy is not ours, and he moves men like George Müller to give of their resources (financial, time, energy, talents) to accomplish the goal. Still others serve the cause in ways like sounding the rallying cry as mobilizers in the home country and praying until their knees are worn out and their hearts are saturated with the same passion. The question now is what can you do about it? What intentional choice for purposeful involvement will you make?

Consider the six ways of involvement listed on page 199. OMF International would love to talk with you more about how God is calling and equipping you to become more involved. Throughout East Asia, billions are still waiting to hear the "glad tidings" that we have known about for centuries. God is not willing that they should perish without his salvation. What part will you play to join him in his pursuit?

CHRONOLOGICAL OUTLINE

1832, May 21. James Hudson Taylor born in Barnsley, Yorkshire, England.

1849, June. Conversion, followed by call to life service.

1850, May. Beginning medical studies in Hull as assistant to Dr. Robert Hardey.

1853, Sep. 19. Sailed for China, as a missionary with the Chinese Evangelization Society.

1850-1864. The Taiping Rebellion.

1854, March 1. Hudson Taylor landed in Shanghai.

1854-1855. Ten evangelistic journeys.

1855, Oct.-Nov. First home "inland": six weeks on the island of Tsungming.

1855-1856. Seven months with the Rev. William C. Burns.

1856, Oct. Settlement at Ningpo.

1857, June. Resignation from the Chinese Evangelization Society.

1858, Jan. 20. Marriage to Maria J. Dyer.

1859, Sep. Took charge of Dr. George Parker's hospital, Ningpo.

1860, Summer. Return to England on first furlough.

1860-1865. Hidden years.

1865, June 25. Surrender at Brighton, and prayer for 24 fellow workers for inland China.

1866, May. Lammermuir party sails to China.

1866, Dec. Settlement of the Lammermuir party in Hangchow.

1867, Aug. 23. Death of little Gracie, Hudson and Maria Taylor's daughter.

1868, Aug. 22. The Yangchow Riot.

1869, Sep. 4. Entered into the "exchanged life": "God has made me a new man!"

1870, July 23. Death of Maria Taylor (née Dyer).

1872, Mar. Retirement of William and Mary Berger.

1872, Aug. 6. Formation of the London Council of the China Inland Mission.

1872, Oct. 9. Return to China with Jenny Taylor (née Faulding).

1874, Jan. 27. Recorded prayer for pioneer missionaries for the nine unevangelized provinces.

1874, June. Opening, with Charles Judd, the western branch of the mission in Wuchang.

1874, July 26. Death of Emily Blatchley.

1874-1875, Winter. The lowest ebb: Taylor laid aside in England, paralyzed.

1875, Jan. Appeal for prayer for 18 pioneers for the nine unevangelized provinces.

1876, Sep. 13. Signing of the Chefoo Convention.

1876-1878. Widespread evangelistic journeys throughout inland China.

1878, Autumn. Jenny Taylor leads the advance of women missionaries to the far interior.

1879, Autumn. Mrs. George Nicoll and Mrs. George (Fanny) Clarke pioneer the way for women's work in western China.

1881, May. Death of Emily King, at Hanchung.

1881, Nov. The appeal for "The Seventy" (Wuchang).

1885, Feb. 5. Going out of the "Cambridge Seven."

1886, Nov. 13-26. First meeting of the China Council, and appeal for "The Hundred" (Anking).

1887, Dec. Visit to England of Henry W. Frost, inviting Hudson Taylor to the United States.

1888, Summer. Hudson Taylor's first visit to North America.

1889, Oct. The widest outlook of his life: To Every Creature.

1889, Nov. First visits to Sweden, Norway and Denmark.

1890, Aug. First visit to Australia.

1900, May. Beginning of the Boxer Rebellion.

1900, Aug. D. E. Hoste appointed as acting general director.

1902, Nov. Hudson Taylor resigned directorate to D. E. Hoste.

1904, July 30. Jenny Taylor's death in Switzerland.

1905, Feb. Hudson Taylor's return to China on last visit.

1905, June 3. Home-call from Hunan, Hudson Taylor's death.

1927. Call for 200 more workers.

1930. Policy of self-government for churches.

1934. John and Betty Stam executed in Anhui Province.

1949. Communists take over China.

1949. Sending out of 49 new workers despite increased pressures.

1950-1952. CIM withdraws from China. Work starts in other countries.

1964. CIM's name changes to Overseas Missionary Fellowship (OMF).

1970s and **1980**s. Chinese church reaches 21.5 million baptized members.

1988. First Christian professionals sent into China.

1989. Outreach begins to Asians in the West.

1990s. Outreach to six more creative-access nations.

1993. Name change to OMF International.

1998. Focus on the Buddhist world.

2006. Dr. Patrick Fung, appointed as first Asian director, gives "Call for 900" workers by 2011.

2010. By October 28, 2010, 499 new members, affiliates and associates have joined the fellowship since 2006. OMF International has nearly 3,000 from 36 nations working from home side offices and throughout East Asia.

OMF International
www.omf.org/us

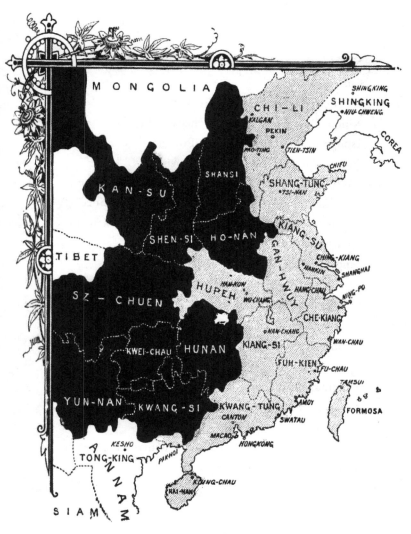

MAP SHOWING THE NINE UNEVANGELISED PROVINCES IN BLACK.

CITY AND PROVINCE NAMES

GLOSSARY TERMS

Taiping Rebellion 1851-64

During the mid-nineteenth century, China's problems were compounded by natural calamities of unprecedented proportions, including droughts, famines, and floods. Government neglect of public works was in part responsible for this and other disasters, and the Qing administration did little to relieve the widespread misery caused by them. Economic tensions, military defeats at Western hands, and anti-Manchu sentiments all combined to produce widespread unrest, especially in the south. South China had been the last area to yield to the Qing conquerors and the first to be exposed to Western influence. It provided a likely setting for the Taiping Rebellion, the largest uprising in modern Chinese history.

Source: www-chaos.umd.edu/history/modern2.html

Treaty of Tientsin/Tianjin

Several documents titled "Treaty of Tientsin" were signed in Tianjin in June 1858, ending the first part of the Second Opium War (1856-1860). France, England, Russia and the United States were the parties involved. These treaties opened eleven more Chinese ports to the foreigners, permitted foreign legations in Beijing, allowed Christian missionary activity, and legalized the import of opium. They were ratified by the Emperor of China in the Beijing Convention of 1860, after the end of the war.

Source: http://en.wikipedia.org/wiki/Treaty_of_Tianjin

Chefoo Convention

A treaty between the Qing and British empires, which was signed in Chefoo on August 21, 1876. The official reason for the treaty was to resolve the "Margary Affair," but the final treaty included a number of items that had no direct relation to the killing of Augustus Raymond Margary the year earlier. One practical result of the treaty was that the official mission of apology to Britain, led by Guo Songtao, became a permanent diplomatic mission in Britain, opening the way for a permanent foreign representation of China.

Source: http://en.wikipedia.org/wiki/Chefoo_Convention

Massacre of Tientsin

Many Chinese scholars and followers of China's many religions resented the white Christian missionaries who had flocked to China in the mid-19th century, and to stir up the common people they frequently circulated rumors that the foreigners were sorcerers. The French Sisters of Charity at their orphanage in the city of Tientsin (Tianjin) used to give small cash rewards to people who brought in homeless or unwanted children, which gave rise to the rumor that children were being abused, kidnapped and used for witchcraft. On June 21, 1870, an angry Chinese crowd led by a local magistrate stood outside the orphanage; the French consul ordered his guards to fire on the mob to disperse it. Enraged by this, the Chinese stormed and sacked the orphanage, killing 18 foreigners, including the consul and 10 nuns. A storm of protest issued from both Paris and Rome, and Western naval ships sailed to Tientsin. France demanded severe punishment for those responsible; 16 Chinese were executed, and China officially apologized to France.

Source: http://www.onwar.com/aced/data/charlie/china1870.htm

Keswick Teaching

The Keswick movement is distinctly evangelical in character, and is supported chiefly by the Evangelical branch of the Church of England. The Keswick speakers and teachers, some 50 in number, are conservative in spirit, clinging to old truths and avoiding new and strange doctrines. Without exception they hold to the absolute plenary inspiration of the Holy Scriptures in every part. To them the Bible is the final court of appeal in matters both of faith and duty. In the Keswick teaching stress is laid upon the infilling of the

Spirit, and upon the power of faith to claim promised blessings. The convention takes an active interest in missions and maintains a number of 322 missionaries in foreign fields.

Source:http://www.ccel.org/s/schaff/encyc/encyc06/htm/iii.lxiv.x.htm

The Keswick teaching is often shared at Keswick conventions, annual gatherings of evangelical Christians in Keswick, in the English county of Cumbria.

The Keswick Convention began in 1875 as a catalyst and focal point for the emerging Higher Life movement in the United Kingdom. A frequent speaker in the early years of the Keswick Convention was Hudson Taylor, founder of the China Inland Mission. Amy Carmichael heard Taylor speak there and decided to dedicate her life to missionary work.

It was Stephen Olford who introduced Billy Graham to the Keswick message at a Keswick Convention in 1946 over a period of days of Bible study and prayer in a hotel room. This teaching gave Billy Graham the assurance of God's power in his life, which Billy said in his autobiography, Just As I Am, came to him as a second blessing, and which has empowered his preaching ever since.

Source: http://en.wikipedia.org/wiki/Keswick_Convention

The Boxer Rebellion

Throughout the nineteenth century, foreigners took control of China and forced the people to make humiliating concessions. A secret society in northern China began a campaign of terror against Christian missionaries and Chinese converts. Foreigners called them "Boxers" because they practiced martial arts and calisthenic rituals. The Boxers believed they had magical powers and that bullets could not harm them. The society wanted to overthrow the Qing Dynasty and expel all foreigners and foreign influences.

The empress dowager publicly opposed the Boxers, but her ministers quietly convinced them to join forces in order to drive foreigners from

China. In the early months of 1900, thousands of Boxers roamed the countryside, attacking Christians. When an international force of 2,100 soldiers attempted to land in China, the empress dowager ordered her imperial army to stop the foreign troops. Throughout the summer of 1900 the Boxers burned churches and foreign residences and killed nearly 32,000 Chinese Christians and more than 100 Protestant missionaries.

Source: http://www.mrdowling.com/613-boxer.html

6 WAYS TO REACH GOD'S WORLD

ARE YOU PURPOSEFULLY INVOLVED IN GOD'S GLOBAL PLAN?

OMF International is pleased to offer a newly revised booklet called *Six Ways to Reach God's World* which describes six ways to be Christ's loving hands in the world: going, praying, sending, mobilizing, welcoming and learning. This is not a new idea. Other organizations and missions-minded people have similar descriptions. However one tries to capture this idea, it is clear that we as Christians need to find our roles in God's redemptive plan. Would God have you engage more deeply in one of these?

1. **Learn**. No matter where we are on the mission journey, we all need to learn more of God's heart and purposes for the world. "Goers" educate themselves on the people and places where they will go. Senders observe carefully to meet the needs of the missionaries. Intercessors learn all they can because "informed prayer is effective prayer." Welcomers build bridges when they know and understand the internationals near them, and mobilizers are most effective as they stay abreast of just what God is doing in the world.

2. **Pray**. Far from a "minor" or "default" role in missions, prayer is essential to the work God does in the world. Intercessors lift the "goers" and the people whom they serve before the throne of God. James (J. O.) Fraser, an OMF missionary to the Lisu of China in the early 1900s, said this about prayer: "Paul may plant and Apollos water, but it is God who gives the increase; and this increase can be brought down from heaven by believing prayer, whether offered in China or in England. ... If this is so, then Christians at home can do as much for foreign missions as those actually on the field. ... What I covet more than anything else is earnest, believing prayer."

3. **Go**. Some people are "goers" who give up the life they have always known, perhaps "creature comforts" or professional opportunities of which they had always dreamed, in exchange for a life in a new culture among people who speak a different language, eat different foods and usually have a much lower standard of living—in order to be conduits of Jesus' love. It may be for a few weeks or a lifetime, but without those willing to step out in faith, the nations will not receive the gospel.

4. **Send**. Since the time of the Apostle Paul, missionaries haven't just gone; they have been sent (see Rom. 10:15). They have been supported and encouraged by God's people. Sending involves giving financially to meet the needs of the mission, but it does not mean one has to be wealthy to give. Senders pray fervently, communicate, lend cars, organize events, print and distribute prayer letters and a wide variety of other creative actions. A "goer" without senders may as well stay home.

5. **Welcome**. In many ways, the world is coming to us. The presence of internationals living in our communities provides a golden opportunity to share the gospel and show the love of Christ. Someone from an "unreached" people group may live right next door. Welcomers join these lives with their own in Christ's name.

6. **Mobilize**. Before one goes, sends, or becomes a prayer partner, he must be mobilized. He must be educated, made aware, motivated and moved to the point of involvement. Once vision is caught, it usually can't be contained. Mobilizers understand that the massive job cannot get done alone, but together, each filling his role, peoples without Jesus will receive the saving message of his gospel.

To learn more, visit *www.6ways2reach.org.*